Vision

Vision

The First Critical Step in Developing a Strategy for Educational Technology

Darryl Vidal and Michael Casey

ROWMAN & LITTLEFIELD
Lanham • Boulder • New York • London

Published by Rowman & Littlefield
A wholly owned subsidiary of The Rowman & Littlefield Publishing Group, Inc.
4501 Forbes Boulevard, Suite 200, Lanham, Maryland 20706
www.rowman.com

Unit A, Whitacre Mews, 26–32 Stannery Street, London SE11 4AB

Copyright © 2014 by Darryl Vidal and Michael Casey

All rights reserved. No part of this book may be reproduced in any form or by any electronic or mechanical means, including information storage and retrieval systems, without written permission from the publisher, except by a reviewer who may quote passages in a review.

British Library Cataloguing in Publication Information Available

Library of Congress Cataloging-in-Publication Data

Vidal, Darryl, 1963–
A vision : the first critical step in developing a strategy for educational technology / Darryl Vidal and Michael Casey.
  pages cm
ISBN 978-1-4758-1211-4 (cloth) — ISBN 978-1-4758-1212-1 (pbk.) — ISBN 978-1-4758-1213-8 (electronic)
1. Educational technology. 2. School management and organization—United States—Decision making. I. Casey, Michael, 1957– II. Title.
LB1028.3.V524 2014
371.33—dc23
                    2014023935

Contents

Foreword		vii
1	The Impetus for Creating an Education Technology Vision	1
2	Crafting the Vision: Let's Get Started	7
3	The Impact of Technology in Education	33
4	Technology Platforms	39
5	Classrooms	59
6	Infrastructure	65
7	Support and Sustainability	75
Conclusion: Vision: Final Thoughts		79
About the Authors		83

Foreword

Today's high school graduates need to be prepared to compete in a highly technical workforce. Our job at Murrieta Valley Unified School District is to ensure that Murrieta Valley students succeed—whether that means getting into college or landing a good-paying job directly after graduation. As academic standards continue to rise, the educational technology revolution is creating exciting opportunities for teaching and learning. Our goal is simple: to provide an educational setting with the advanced technology and skills training needed to succeed in college and future careers. By dedicating our instructional resources to stay aligned with the technology change curve, we will better prepare Murrieta students for college and careers in fields such as science, engineering, technology, and skilled trades.

Our district has launched an educational technology initiative to address these critical issues. Rather than deploy a lot of technology, we intentionally took a step back. We asked many questions: What is our goal? What are we trying to accomplish? What do the many stakeholders we support feel about it?

There is certainly a rush to get technology into the hands of students and staff. This is understandable in today's world. Students are using technology every day to communicate. Academic standards continue to change, and technology plays an increasingly important role. We have deployed a number of new technologies to support student learning. However, as we have implemented certain focused technologies, we have discovered that actual data-based results are important. Does this technology indeed improve student learning? How do we know? Are there multiyear data to support it?

Initiatives such as one-to-one (1:1) are very popular. While we have never disagreed with any particular initiative, we have always felt that technology should take a support role in student learning and not be the driving factor.

Darryl Vidal and Mike Casey's new book has been key for us as we have looked at our technology initiatives. We have followed the processes suggested in the book, developing our own model based on the guidelines proposed here and coming up with our own unique vision for technology—"MVUSD 360." Rather than create a separate vision for technology, we crafted our vision for technology under the umbrella of our already-adopted and time-honored strategic plan. Our board's plan was developed through a long process with a lot of community input; it reflects the values and tenets that are key to our educational community. Technology is not separate or above the goals for the district, so the vision needs to follow our established vision for the district.

I recommend this approach to educational technology leaders at all levels.

Patrick Kelley
Superintendent, Murrieta Valley Unified School District

CHAPTER 1

The Impetus for Creating an Education Technology Vision

There are a number of factors that could lead you to create a vision for technology for your organization. For some organizations, there may be a state or federal requirement to include a vision as a section of an application for funding; for others, a vision may be needed to comply with state or federal guidelines. Most states require schools to have a technology plan to receive or even be eligible for certain types of funding.

Another reason could be that you are applying for a grant or an endowment that requires your organization to have a technology plan with a vision. Perhaps you are the new superintendent or CEO in your organization. Within the first few months of your tenure it would be critical to create and share your vision for the organization and how technology is a part of that vision. It would be important to communicate that vision to support any changes you want to initiate as well as to reinforce the ongoing efforts of the organization.

Board members may be asking for the district's vision, as it is a basic part of any large organization. Board members are members of the local community. They often receive e-mails, phone calls, and other communication from their constituents. They see their neighbors, and they run into folks when they are out in public—whether in formal settings, such as a board meeting, or something as casual as the local market or soccer field. Board members need to be able to communicate the district's vision. It helps them explain what the school district is all about in an all-encompassing statement and gives them a tool to support the organization and its initiatives.

RESPONSIBILITY FOR THE VISION

No matter the reason for wanting to create a vision or to revisit your existing vision, there is really only one person responsible for driving the effort: the superintendent. The superintendent needs to guide the ship and put together the right team of people to help craft a vision that will support all the efforts of the district related to technology and the district's strategic plan.

Could another player direct the project? Of course, the instructional assistant superintendent or the chief information officer may be the true initiator of the effort, but the direction must come from the top down. The cabinet must have an intimate understanding of the entire concept and reinforce it throughout the organization in meetings and communications.

When the entire leadership team acts in concert, the influence will naturally permeate the organization. When no dissension exists among the leaders there will be less support for grassroots resistance. That does not mean that such resistance will not happen. That is why the vision must be focused but generally popular enough to achieve widespread support.

HOW THE VISION SUPPORTS THE ORGANIZATION

A well-written education technology vision can support an organization in a number of ways. At first, you may think that the only reason to have a vision is to fulfill some sort of requirement for funding or to appease board members or the public. Although those reasons may be accurate, let's examine a few other ways that the vision supports your organization. You might be surprised.

Focus

Having a vision can help your organization stay focused. It lets everyone know what you are thinking. It tells people where the organization is going. It is the overall purpose for what you do. In any complex organization, it is easy to lose focus. Having a vision and communicating it effectively will help all your stakeholders and subordinates think about what they are doing and how their actions are aligned with the vision. Leaders may actively practice this by testing the basis for their decisions and using the vision as a tool in communications—continually aligning the organization to it.

Validates Actions

How many times have you heard these questions: Who made that decision? Why are they purchasing those computers? Why can't we buy what we want? Why does that department get to go to conferences? How did you get the budget for that? Where did you get the money? The list goes on and on. There seems to be no end to such questions.

Having a vision may not end these questions, but a vision allows leadership to separate itself from the decision, to let the vision be the reason. Folks will always question and challenge decisions and actions that they do not support or understand. A vision can help an organization refocus and guide team members to understand the actions that were taken.

Supports Long- and Short-Term Decision Making

Having a vision will help guide the decision makers in the organization. Whether the decisions have a big or small impact on the organization, whether they are strategic or tactical, all decisions should be "seen" within the vision: "If it is not part of our vision, why are we doing it?" We dig deeper into structured decision-making later in this book, but the vision puts the decision-making factors in front so that many can understand them from the outset.

Digging Out

Oftentimes, people within an organization begin to take actions or make decisions that are not aligned with the vision—it is easy to stray from the vision, to lose focus. There can be many causes: stress, budget, personnel issues, organizational issues, or simply to accomplish another goal. It is natural to forget about the focus of the organization during these times. When things start to go in a different direction, having a vision will help folks refocus, get them back on track, and get them working toward the vision again. If the effort is not part of our vision, then we must ask ourselves why we are doing it.

Funding

We do not always have to be altruistic about having a vision. Having a vision may help secure additional funding or at least ensure eligibility for future funding opportunities.

Proactive Engagement

Having a vision provides the opportunity to be proactive in communicating to your organization's stakeholders. The vision provides leadership with a backdrop and metric for every meeting, communication, and activity. It helps the organization stay focused. It provides a basis for decision making. It can prevent staff from making decisions that do not align with the vision. The vision should be part of the organization's daily lexicon.

HOW THE VISION SUPPORTS INSTRUCTION

Of course, the key idea in developing an educational technology vision is *education*, not *technology*. The vision needs not only to reflect the educational focus but also to embody the essence of what you are attempting to achieve with your instructional practices. We hear a lot about "twenty-first-century learning" and "Common Core standards." How do they fit into your vision? How will you embody the pillars of Common Core and twenty-first-century learning practices?

Somehow your vision needs to weave in the concepts of collaboration, communication, critical thinking, and creativity. If these Common Core precepts are not included in the vision, then how are you supporting instructional practices in your district with the integration of technology?

A lot of school districts have rushed to put technology into students' hands without really having a vision for how these devices support the districts' instructional practices. The current impetus for acquiring technology for student use seems to be Smarter Balanced testing. Although technology tools are required for Smarter Balanced testing and even though the acquisition of technology to support this new testing environment is necessary, how will you use that technology after the testing period? Is there a plan? Will these newly acquired tools support your instructional practice as well as support Smarter Balanced testing?

These are some of the reasons why it is important to include in your educational technology vision the connection to instruction, Common Core, and twenty-first-century learning skills. Without a clear vision that supports instruction, chaos reigns.

COMMUNICATING THE VISION

Once the education technology vision is defined and approved by leadership (don't worry; we show you how to do that in the upcoming chapters), the next critical step is to communicate your vision effectively throughout the organization to all stakeholders. Everyone should know, understand, and be able to communicate the vision. In fact, the process and method of communicating the vision is an opportunity to demonstrate the organization's commitment to this new vision. If the vision is simply included in an e-mail, then staff will conclude that it holds a similar level of importance. If the vision is presented by district leaders in an "all-hands" meeting, the organization will see and hear the commitment and dedication to this new edict.

Watching and listening to the superintendent give the background and salient points of these important tenets weaves the vision into the organization's fabric. As leadership revisits and refers to the vision for guidance, the organization will follow the lead. Similarly, if after this initial communication, leaders go off in different directions or, worse yet, undermine the vision through either words or action, the vision will become stale and lose credence. Thus, district leaders must continually refer to and use the vision to guide their daily interactions and decision making.

Everyone in your organization should be able to describe the vision and how it guides the organization's technology endeavors. In fact, the vision cannot be overcommunicated. It should be reflected in all the various ways that your organization communicates: on the header of your website, on business cards, on letterhead and stationery, and so on. Excerpts of your vision could also become the subtitle of your e-mail signature.

CHAPTER 2

Crafting the Vision
Let's Get Started

Crafting a vision is the first critical step in developing an educational technology plan or strategic plan for technology. Many organizations have yet to develop a discrete process for developing an educational technology vision based on curricular objectives. Oftentimes such a vision is based on technology-based initiatives, such as one-to-one (1:1) computing, Bring Your Own Device (BYOD), or "anytime, anyplace" computing.

Vision: The First Critical Step in Developing a Strategy for Educational Technology is intended to define a process for educational administrators and leaders to develop a vision for educational technology. This book will examine real-world examples and provide a systematic approach to engaging the appropriate stakeholders, identifying precepts and tenets, and organizing these into a vision that can be used to communicate the educational technology identity of your district or school.

This book is not intended to provide your district with its vision. Rather, the purpose is to provide you and your staff with the inquiry process and building blocks to aid your organization in developing a vision. This vision then can be communicated to all stakeholders, from the board of education to the classroom teacher, and can bring all parties to the same source of inspiration—so they will be marching to the same drum. If this process is done effectively, not only will all of the stakeholders see where they, or their departments, fit within the vision, they will also understand how to support the vision from their particular role in the organization.

What is a vision? How is it different from a mission, values, goals, or strategy?

- *Vision.* A thought, concept, or object formed by the imagination.
- *Mission.* A specific task with which a person or a group is charged.
- *Values.* The ideals, customs, institutions, etc., of a society toward which the people of the group have an affective regard.
- *Strategy.* A combination of the ends (goals) for which the firm is striving and the means (policies) by which it is seeking to get there.[1]

The interesting and not-so-obvious part of this is that the vision is often presumed—we all just assume that we're thinking the same thing or have the same goals and objectives. So it is not surprising that almost every book or lesson on planning—whether it be about education, business, or building a soapbox-derby car—calls for defining goals and objectives and developing mission statements. The vision is left out, or not addressed specifically, even though it is the guiding tenet for the mission, goals, objectives, and strategy.

There is a danger in not undergoing a formal process of developing a vision. If all stakeholders do not have consensus on a central tenet, departments and individuals may go off in different directions—basing their efforts and decisions on their own departmental wants and needs. When you get to the end, did you really get what everyone wanted?

There is a cartoon that has been circulating since the 1960s in the United Kingdom that illustrates a good example of not everyone having the same vision (see Fig. 2.1).

When was the last time a plan was presented to your leadership, and someone asked, "Who made that decision?" Or someone said, "That's never going to work because. . . ." These statements are symptoms of not having everyone on board through the development process—not sharing the same vision. When these statements are made during the communication process, they only serve to undermine the new edict.

In the vision and strategic planning development processes, it is ultimately important to have *all* stakeholders involved not only in the kickoff and initial meetings but in every iteration of the process.

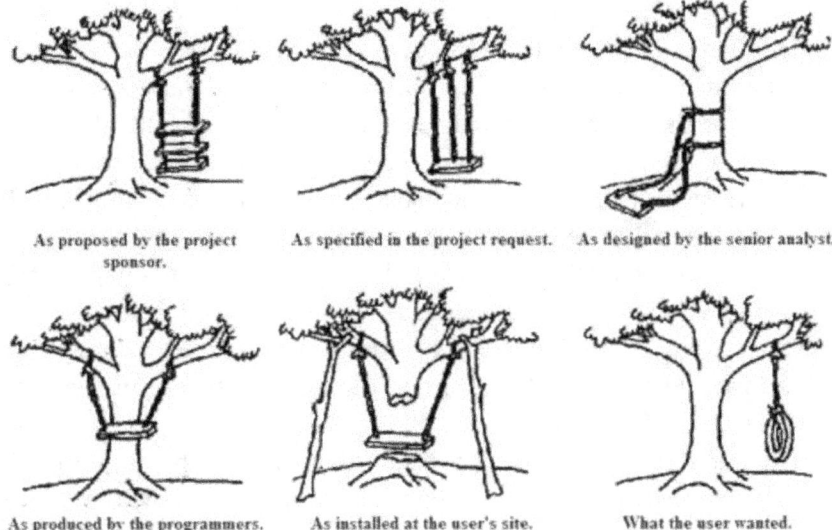

Figure 2.1

All stakeholders must understand how and why the vision and plan developed as it did. That way, when the formal presentation is delivered, everyone knows how that decision was made and who made it.

When all leadership looks and acts to be in support of the vision, the subordinates will naturally follow suit. When department heads communicate the vision to subordinates—although they may not agree—they will understand the motivation and impetus driving the decision-making process.

What you don't need is a department head—possibly the information technology (IT) director—saying things like, "You're not going to like this, but this is what they came up with." Or, "I know this isn't going to work, but here's their plan." This type of dissention and dissociation breeds more of the same by subordinates and then bleeds through the organization.

By getting all department heads to understand and be an integral part of the development process, even if just by attending meetings, it becomes more difficult for them to dissociate themselves from the outcome.

Similarly, it also becomes difficult for them to sit in these meetings without voicing concerns or raising objections as they are encountered.

And it will be necessary that these concerns and objections receive specific attention through the process—not necessarily compromise, capitulation, or appeasement, but documented consideration.

Think of the many times that planning meetings are held and the IT director cannot attend because "the network is down" or a similar emergency arises. Or the assistant superintendent cannot attend because a critical issue came up at a school site.

Truth be told, the IT director shouldn't be the one fixing the network anyway; that's what the engineers are supposed to be doing.

This type of dissociation leads again to those deadly comments: "Who made that decision?" or "I don't know how they came up with that."

If the educational technology vision development process doesn't involve leadership and their subordinates, the vision will be dead before it is born.

Choosing the person to lead the development process is as important as the final outcome—possibly even more. The process must be formal and methodical. The deliverables should include a formal presentation and a final set of educational technology vision statements.

Finally, an all-encompassing yet simple graphic should seal the deal—we all know how charts and graphs can aid in communicating any message.

Any formal planning process must be interactive and iterative, and the facilitator must gain consensus at every step.

This is one reason that engaging an outside resource to help with this development process may be critical. The facilitator must be a trusted resource. They must be beyond reproach, credible, and above departmental politics. They must be able to enforce the needs of the process.

While we are engaged for this purpose, it is important not to let individuals hijack the process. The facilitator must be able to keep the process on track and keep the participants focused.

If the assistant superintendent of instruction leads the process and the IT director doesn't participate, or vice versa—well, we've already told you what happens. There is no bigger waste of time than having one staff member take on such an important role only to have their peers sabotage the process because they harbor personal resentments or reservations.

We all know what we are referring to. If the department head escapes from the meeting and goes back to their department and says, "I got out of that stupid meeting, what a waste of time," the process is already ruined.

Departmental agendas cannot be allowed to influence the goals and outcomes of this process.

The facilitator of the development and planning process must avoid these occurrences. Saying "You missed that meeting, therefore your objection doesn't warrant discussion" doesn't allow proper consideration of the issue, and the groundswell of objections starts to arise within the departments.

These types of miscues must be avoided, and meeting attendance must be enforced, once again, by leadership. A superintendent cannot expect school leaders to attend if he or she does not attend the meetings or enforce the attendance of key players. It would be better to postpone and reschedule the meeting for a time when all can attend than to continue developing and presenting a plan that no one agrees with.

Also, when the participants see that the meetings are postponed because they cannot attend, they will realize that their involvement is paramount. This dedication and commitment works both ways.

The vision for educational technology should be in alignment with other district plans, the district strategic plan, the state-mandated technology plan, Title I plans, and Local Control and Accountability Plan (LCAP), to name a few.

- According to the definitions above, mission defines the fundamental purpose of the organization, values define the beliefs of the organization, strategy defines the ends and the means, and goals define objective results. The vision, however, is really the key input to determining each of these subordinate nouns.

The vision seeks to provide inspiration to work toward a simple, generalized result, one that unifies all stakeholders.

Developing a vision requires the organization to look to the future, to think *big*. Google uses the strategy of "10x Thinking."

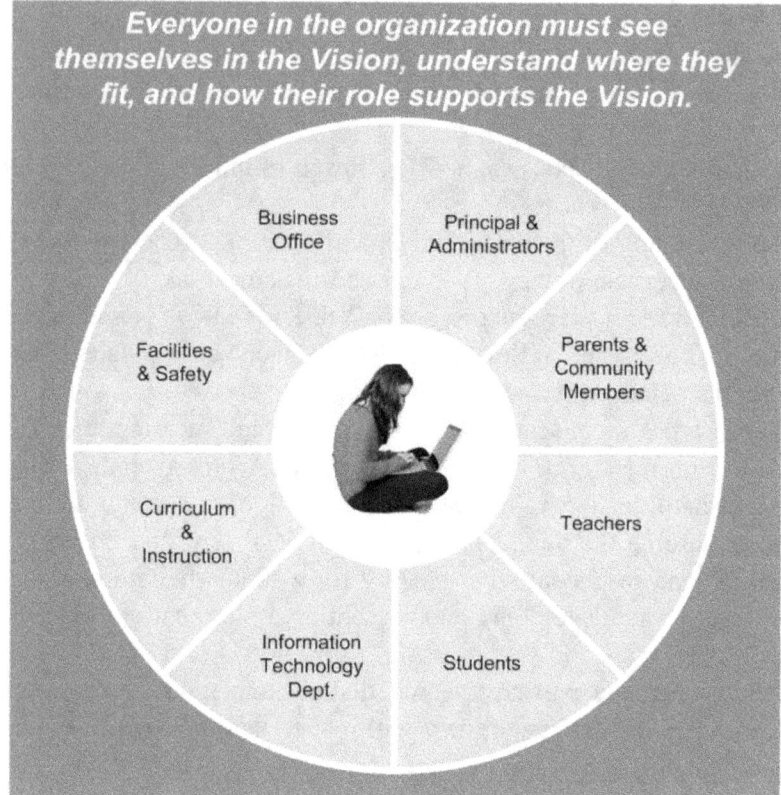

Figure 2.2

Don't just try to make incremental changes; instead, think of making things ten times better. This is also known as the "leapfrog" effect—don't just take the next logical step, take the next ten steps! And they may not seem logical!

So often school districts try only to "catch up" with their neighboring districts. We have actually had superintendents come to us and say, "We want to be just like [fill-in-the-blank] school district."

Adjust your thinking: you really want to be ten times that district!

To do this you will have to advance your district vision by ten times. This may be a difficult task for some. Not everyone in your organization is a visionary! But with the right leadership and opportunity to participate, everyone can provide valuable input and ideas that feed the vision. Go find them and get them on the team.

The chart above attempts to list the stakeholders in the organization. Your organization may have additional or different stakeholders. Whatever the case may be, there are a number of areas that must also be considered.

EDUCATIONAL OPEN SYSTEM INTERCONNECTIONS MODEL (EOSI)

Being technology geeks, we like to build models to create structure around systems. There is a standard technology model that we can modify to support our discussion around visioning and the different areas that we need to consider. The Open Systems Interconnection (OSI) model "characterizes and standardizes the internal functions of a communication system by partitioning it into abstraction layers." We'll personalize

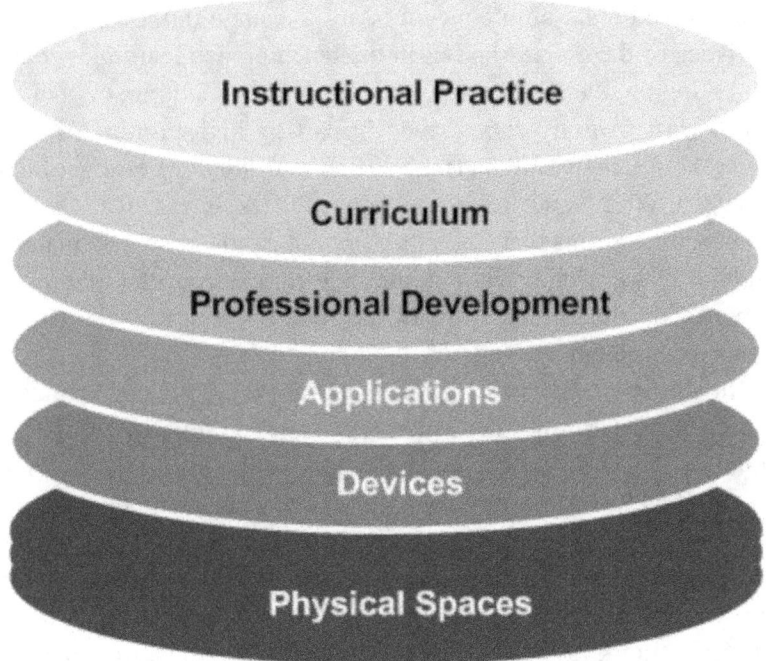

Figure 2.3

the model to meet our needs, show how the different layers fit together, and later show how they fit in with information technology.

From an educational technology viewpoint, the different areas that we need to consider are instructional practice, curriculum, professional development, applications, devices, and physical spaces.

INSTRUCTIONAL PRACTICE

Instructional practice describes strategies for how to teach students the curriculum that has been adopted. Many times more than one instructional practice is used in the teaching of children. We have listed a few of the newest, if not trendiest, practices that are popular today. We don't subscribe to any one practice. We will leave that up to the experts in your school district.

Flipped Classroom

The flipped classroom concept is not a change in the physical characteristics of the classroom but in the teaching and learning pedagogy.

"Flipping the classroom" has become something of a buzzword in the last several years, driven in part by high-profile articles in the *New York Times* (Fitzpatrick, 2012), *Chronicle of Higher Education* (Berrett, 2012), and *Science* (Mazur, 2009). In essence, "flipping the classroom" means that students gain first exposure to new material outside of class, usually via reading or lecture videos, and then use class time to do the harder work of assimilating that knowledge, perhaps through problem solving, discussion, or debates.

In terms of Bloom's revised taxonomy (2001), this means that students are doing the lower levels of cognitive work (gaining knowledge and comprehension) outside of class and focusing on the higher forms of cognitive work (application, analysis, synthesis, and/or evaluation) in class, where they have the support of their peers and instructor. This model contrasts with the traditional model in which "first exposure" occurs via lecture in class, with students assimilating knowledge through homework—thus, the term "flipped classroom."[2]

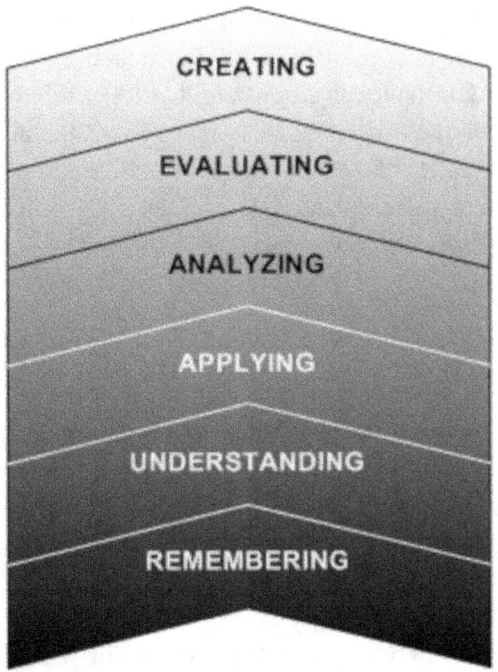

Figure 2.4 Bloom's Taxonomy

Whether the flipping is initiated by the school or teacher, it does require a level of technological expertise and practice. Audio or video lectures are prerecorded and distributed or made available to students using methods or technologies such as podcasts, PowerPoint and multimedia presentations, videos, educational content websites, and the like.

The students must have access to and mastery of these technologies in order to gain this initial exposure. Then, ideally, the teacher can use advanced tools, such as learning management systems (LMS) and/or assessment software to evaluate each student's understanding.

Instructional leaders must determine if this is a site-wide or district-wide initiative, have a keen understanding of the technologies and logistics, and then develop the procurement and professional development models.

Finally, what is the point of an initiative if the results aren't measured and evaluated?

If these details can't be ironed out at the site or district level, then once again it will become the individual teacher's responsibility to work out these details, technologies, and practices. How then does the school determine the efficacy of the endeavor at the classroom level?

The educational technology vision, in this case, must acknowledge the need for these different models and take a position of *allow and enable* or *advocate and implement*.

Virtual Classrooms, Distance Learning, and Remote Students

These concepts are not new—in fact, they are quite old relative to the latest enabling technologies—and they have each been exhaustively discussed and explored in previous writings and research.

The point is that physical distance does not have to be an obstacle to learning. And the educational technology vision does not require this level of specificity unless it is a demographic or geographic need and/or goal.

An examination of various virtual classroom scenarios will aid in modeling solutions that may benefit your classrooms and students. Examples of implementations will help define curriculum models that apply to the various virtual classroom concepts.

As in all curriculum development, objectives define the needs. There should be no virtual classroom application where no need exists.

However, the curriculum, in and of itself, may define the need. For instance, the curriculum may include a "project-based" learning exercise in which statistics students from outlying schools survey each other and develop statistical analysis of results. This activity may use synchronous technologies to support remote participants, as well as asynchronous collaboration tools to facilitate the interaction.

Similarly, there may be no virtual need driven by the curriculum— the need may be inherent in the demographics or geographies of the student base. For instance, a rural district spread over a large region may offer the same curriculum for calculus but have to reach multiple students in outlying schools. Thereby, they need a real physical classroom joined by students located in remote schools.

Finally, is the need or objective to impact a specific core of students within the site or district, or every student in the district? The answer to this question may dictate the need for one technologically enhanced classroom at each site or, alternately, some basic video conferencing, or "hang out" (Google) capability in every classroom.

For instance, will all Science, Technology, Engineering, and Math (STEM) students utilize a video collaboration and sharing curriculum that includes remote users? This would require access to the video collaboration applications in only STEM classrooms. Or is this video collaboration curriculum implemented for all middle school students, requiring the equipment and infrastructure in middle schools only?

To understand the virtual classroom concepts, it is helpful to review the capabilities of the traditional classroom—what we refer to as the "bricks-and-mortar" classroom.

The virtual classroom is identical in concept to the bricks-and-mortar classroom in that the facility itself supports all nature of curriculum and classroom instruction models. There is no limit to which concepts or subject matter can be studied within the classroom walls.

In order to understand the virtual classroom, let us first examine the bricks-and-mortar classroom. Within the traditional bricks-and-mortar classroom, the following are the case:

- You may have any combination of teachers and students, and the fundamental activity within the classroom is generally leader led.
- The teacher can interact and communicate with the students using all methods, including speech, visuals, models, examples, texts, audio, and video.
- The students can interact with each other.
- The schedules of the teachers and students are synchronized—that is, to have a class, all teachers and students must be in the classroom *at the same time.*

Now, let's look at the characteristics of the virtual classroom. The virtual classroom can transcend the bricks-and-mortar classroom in one or two ways:

1. Expanding the synchronous interactivity beyond the bricks-and-mortar classroom by adding remote participants

2. Implementing tools for asynchronous content and interactivity that allow for the recording and cataloging of content, such as video streams or podcasts

For instance, a session-recording capability would allow each class session taught to be recorded and then reviewed at a later date. As the class recordings are indexed and archived, an entire curriculum can be compiled to support self-paced online learning—remote or local.

Synchronous Teaching and Learning

Synchronous learning is teaching and learning happening at the same time—simultaneously. There are specific characteristics that still make synchronous learning better than any asynchronous model.

Primarily, there is a higher level of physical and communicative interaction between the teacher and students, and among the students themselves.

Close physical proximity is still more engaging than viewing others on televisions or projector screens.

> Physical proximity of workers in an office usually yields a high level of casual, serendipitous, spontaneous, non-intrusive communications among office staff. Communications between people who are nearby can be more easily synchronized to times when all parties are mentally ready to focus on the communications.[3]

The classroom students and teachers are similarly affected by intimate verbal and nonverbal interaction. Individuals are stimulated by gesture, nuance, smell, and low-level auditory signals from all participants.

We'll discuss virtual classrooms and distance learning in much more detail later in this book. At this level, it is most important to understand if there is a demographic or geographic need for these models to be part of the vision.

Asynchronous Technology Tools

Asynchronous tools for learning have been around since the beginning of time in the form of textbooks and written content and materials.

My high school science teacher "flipped" his classroom more than forty years ago by telling us, "Your homework is to read chapter 2 before you come to class tomorrow because we'll discuss it, then take a quiz." Today the flipped classroom assignment might look more like this:

> At home tonight, view the Khan Academy video on adding fractions with unlike denominators. After viewing the video, download the worksheet and work on problems one through four. Then in class tomorrow we will review problems one through four and answer any questions you have.

Only in the last few decades has audio recording via cassette or CD become more widespread, but even then, the cassette or CD was loaned out to students who missed the lecture rather than to all the students, because the teacher was not about to make 150 copies of it.

In the last decade we've seen podcasting as a fleeting "hot" trend in asynchronous learning.

The instructional impact, not much more than technology augmentation, has been limited to using a widely available and portable listening device in the form of the iPod or an audio stream via the Internet.

But podcasting has not really added much more than simplifying asynchronous audio playback and maybe some "push" technology to make distribution via e-mail or the web (through an RSS feed) easier.

We've all heard many podcasting examples and anecdotes, but rarely have we seen a school-wide or district-wide adoption of podcasting as a curricular model. And more importantly, these examples don't consistently result in higher test scores.

For example, five years ago (circa 2009) podcasting was a popular method of delivering asynchronous audio content, but the distribution and assessment aspects were not integrated through the exercise.

The delivery tool for the podcast was not integrated with the assessment tool. The teacher still had to collect test results and enter grades into the gradebook, and the school did not have a vast library of all the year's podcasts for all teachers. Moreover, not all students necessarily had iPods either.

A simple Google search for podcasting and improved test scores resulted in no specific supporting research:

The Effects of Different Podcasting Strategies on Student Achievement in a Large, College Level Inquiry Biology Course

Although this study found that podcasting did not significantly affect student percent gain scores, the benefit of podcasting on student attitude appears to be an effect. Students consistently have a very positive attitude towards podcasting and courses that offer it. Evans (2008) found that students felt podcasts were a better study tool than their text or even their own notes. In this study 68% of students reported that podcasts were a valuable resource, while 80% of students liked having podcasts available. If podcasts did not provide some degree of benefit, one would expect the percentage of satisfied students to be lower than what was reported. However, if podcasts were as valuable as students insist, why did many of these same students use less than half the available podcasts while 38% report discontinuing their use at some point during the semester? (Tarren John Shaw, Oklahoma State University, December 2009)

But today (circa 2014) we truly are seeing a revolution in asynchronous technology tools in the form of streaming video (and audio), mobility, device independence, and the most significant features of the traditionally synchronous benefits of collaboration and interactivity. In essence, we are seeing synchronous features and benefits brought to the asynchronous model.

Cloud-based interactive content allows teachers to do the following:

- Develop media-rich video content available to the student, anywhere, on any device
- View and explore content
- Use media-rich tools (video and audio recording via webcam) to comment and evaluate
- Compile these media streams to offer asynchronous collaboration and assessment

This suite of functions and capabilities is enabled through standardized formats and devices, massive Internet bandwidth and wireless saturation, and comprehensive (cloud-based) learning management systems that allow the teachers to categorize, manage, and distribute media-rich curriculum.

Today, the whole cycle—curriculum development, cataloging, distribution, delivery, execution, assessment, reporting, and archiving—is now available in most learning environments.

Imagine being able to have all students view a video exercise, produce and record video comments and responses, view other students' videos, and collaborate through this process as the responses accumulate, then imagine the teacher being able to assess responses and interact through this system to individual students or the entire class, all via asynchronous video!

The back-end LMS is storing and managing the content and assessments. The student's own device or 1:1 device is the delivery mechanism. The school's or district's wireless and Internet connectivity is providing all the bandwidth and connectivity. Why isn't your school or district providing these tools now?

The virtual classroom models, supported by appropriate technologies, make these models more and more complex, truly requiring detailed examination of the curricular and physical need in order to address them with specificity and avoid the risk of spending a lot of money for the wrong learning models and inappropriate technologies.

Imagine procuring and installing a video conferencing interface (VCI) to enable remote students when the remote students don't all have Internet access from home. Or building teaching walls with interactive whiteboards (IWB) and realizing that the primary students cannot reach the IWB.

In one example, a school district procured a high-end video conferencing system to enable a calculus course to be taught in two high schools by one teacher—there were not enough students in one high school to warrant the class.

However, the class failed to occur the first year because the two schools could not synchronize their schedules.

In the second year, after a hard-fought scheduling war, the class was taught over the VCI, and it was successful. In fact, the system was designed so the teacher was able to teach the class from either location.

However, in the third year the class was dropped in the one location because of lack of students. Currently the system is only used for administrative meetings.

CURRICULUM

Curriculum is about what we are going to teach. Most states have adopted standards that we strive to achieve. More recently, many states have adopted Common Core standards, which were developed nationwide (www.corestandards.org).

School districts often adopt materials to support their instruction of the Common Core. Whether textbooks, consumable guides, online curriculum, or other support materials, there are a lot of choices that support Common Core.

In developing your vision you need to be sure that all of the stakeholders in your group know and understand what curriculum you are using and how it supports your strategies to achieve Common Core state standards.

PROFESSIONAL DEVELOPMENT

Professional development is the cornerstone for the success of any technology initiative. We recommend that 20 percent of the total cost of implementing a new technology be used for professional development.

Even though you are implementing some form of new technology, your professional development effort should be less about the technology and more about how to use the technology effectively to support instruction.

For example, in a recent implementation of Chromebooks at a school district, we allocated forty hours professional development per teacher for this particular rollout. The breakdown of the hours for professional development was as follows:

0.5 hours	Device
39.5 hours	Curriculum Integration

Most devices today are rather intuitive to learn. It's not like the old days when you had to know which DIP switches to set on an interface card to make the computer print.

Most of your time should be focused on integrating the new tools to support instruction. I actually had a teacher ask me, "Hey, Mike, where is the curriculum we are going to teach using these new Chromebooks?"

My response was, "You will continue to teach the same curriculum that we adopted as a district. All you're going to do is learn how to integrate this new tool to enhance your instructional practice."

So the 39.5 hours allotted for curriculum integration was used to divide teachers into grade-level teams (elementary school), examine the first trimester curriculum, and see where technology could improve the instructional practice.

We started by providing lots of supports for teachers. As a grade-level team we reviewed our first trimester curriculum, thought of ways to enhance instruction through the use of technology, then tried it out in classes.

We observed and critiqued each new technology integration. Then we revised, and we continued this iterative process until we felt we had a great lesson.

APPLICATIONS

Finding the killer app has been a lifelong journey. The key to finding the killer app for your organization is to have a clear understanding of what your curriculum focus is and what your instructional practices are. There are literally millions of applications out there in the marketplace, and new ones pop up every day. Finding the one that best meets your needs may take some time and some trial and error.

When selecting applications, think about trying to future-proof your selections. How do you do this? Look for applications that are hosted online, and by that we mean web-based applications. Web-based applications are not dependent on a specific hardware platform. Web-based applications usually work on a variety of devices: laptops, desktops, tablets, and smartphones. They are updated frequently, and there is no install for the application or its updates.

A few things to look for when searching for an application:

- Look for "tools," such as GAFE (Google Apps for Education), that can be used across all curricular areas.
- What are the fees, if any?
- Was the application written specifically for the web? Or was it "ported over" from a desktop application? Your IT folks can tell the difference. If you don't know, ask them.

- How often is the application updated?
- What is the process for support?
- Do teachers and students need individual passwords or accounts?
- Does the application track student progress?
- Does the application support teacher-student relationships? That is, does a teacher create a "class" and add students into it? If so, the teacher then has control and information about the students in their class for reports, progress, and so on. It also prevents others who have not been invited or are not welcome from joining the class. A couple of good, supportive examples are Edmodo and Teacher Dashboard by Hapara. These support Google Apps for Education.
- Does the app support connections to your IT department's directory services (Active Directory, LDAP, NDS)? This will allow single sign-on. Once again, this is a question your IT department should work with the vendor to understand.

DEVICES

The selection of devices comes *after* you know what your curriculum is, what your instructional practice looks like, and what applications you're going to use to support your curriculum initiatives. Buying devices is an easy decision once you've answered these questions.

Many school districts fall into the trap of buying devices without a plan for how they will be used to support instruction. How many districts can you name that have purchased iPads for every student? What curriculum was this decision based on? How are they managed in the classroom? What professional development was provided? What is the life-cycle cost of the devices?

There are a lot of devices that are on the market, and new ones seem to come out almost every month. We can't predict what new devices will come out a year from now. However, we can say with certainty that they will be *mobile* and *wireless*! And, the web *will* be the method of delivery for applications and information.

There are a number of factors to consider in your decision-making process. Below is a tool that we have used to help in the selection process. It has two main components: *curriculum* and *technology* (Fig. 2.5).

Curriculum

	Low (Bad)		High (Good)		
Student Writing Process—how does the tech tool support. . . .					
Keyboarding	1	2	3	4	NA
Writing and Re-Writing	1	2	3	4	NA
Teacher Review/Comments	1	2	3	4	NA
Peer Review/Comments	1	2	3	4	NA
Google Docs	1	2	3	4	NA
Supports Content Creation and Presentation					
Writing	1	2	3	4	NA
Presentations	1	2	3	4	NA
Sharing	1	2	3	4	NA
Works with projectors	1	2	3	4	NA
Printing Capabilities	1	2	3	4	NA
Students—Are they likely to use this tool . . .					
Ease of User	1	2	3	4	NA
Keyboard Size	1	2	3	4	NA
Monitor Size	1	2	3	4	NA
Would work equitably for all students	1	2	3	4	NA
Supports Adaptive Technology Devices	1	2	3	4	NA
Research—how does this tool support students doing research					
Effective Internet Search Engine tool	1	2	3	4	NA
Performs searches quickly	1	2	3	4	NA
Supports other research tools i.e. dictionaries, thesaurus, etc.	1	2	3	4	NA
Safety and Control features when searching	1	2	3	4	NA

Technology

Durability (Life Cycle)					
Monitor—quality, size, durability, hinges, etc.	1	2	3	4	NA
Keyboard—size appropriate, durable	1	2	3	4	NA
Connectors—USB, projector, ear buds	1	2	3	4	NA
Operating System					
Boot Time—starts up quickly	1	2	3	4	NA
Virus Protection					
Requires Maintenance or Updates	yes			no	NA
Updates					
OS—Requires User or Technician to update	yes			no	NA
Applications—Requires User or Technician to update	yes			no	NA
Maintenance					
OS—Requires routine maintenance	yes			no	NA
Software—Requires routine maintenance	yes			no	NA
Support					
Factory	1	2	3	4	NA
3rd Party	1	2	3	4	NA
Device Remote Management					
Syncing—Device syncs automatically for updates	yes			no	NA
AD—Active Directory is supported	yes			no	NA
Ghost—Device can be 'imaged' using Ghost	yes			no	NA
Web—Device can be managed via a web interface	yes			no	NA
Total Cost of Ownership	1	2	3	4	NA

Figure 2.5 Student Technology Tool Evaluation. Comments: We recommend that a tool like this be used by both the Curriculum and Technology leaders in your district. A tool like this will help to take some of the emotion out of the buying decision. You need to make sure that the devices you select support instruction and you have the staff and resources to support them for their life-span.

PHYSICAL AND VIRTUAL SPACES

As we begin to look at learning spaces, there are some precepts that should be considered.

First, we do not know what technologies will emerge in the future. However, we can predict with confidence that the technologies will be mobile and wireless.

Second, the traditional learning spaces that we have today were designed with neither mobile technologies in mind nor the need for high-speed wireless connectivity. Ergo, they are no longer effective learning spaces and do not support twenty-first-century learning activities of collaboration, communication, creativity, critical thinking, and the presentation of authentic work of students.

Third, our learning spaces require flexibility. One hour the teacher may want students sitting in traditional rows, another part of the day they may need to work independently, and yet another time they will need to work in collaborative learning groups.

This will require furniture that is movable, flexible, and reconfigurable with little or no effort. It is amazing that when we discuss all the great ideas around twenty-first-century learning spaces and what they might look like, we are really talking about furniture—not technology.

It's funny that we need to rediscover the wheel! Literally—furniture with wheels (casters).

Fourth, research shows that when students are responsible for designing their own learning spaces and can do so based on the task at hand, they are much more productive.

Keeping these four precepts in mind, there are a number of ways people have labeled learning spaces. One interesting study by the University of Minnesota's Office of Information Technology investigates the impact of active-learning spaces on both faculty and students.

This is what they found:

- Faculty teaching in new learning spaces and students learning in them both had strongly positive attitudes toward the spaces at the end of the term.
- Both faculty and students perceived reduced psychological distance between faculty and students, and among students.

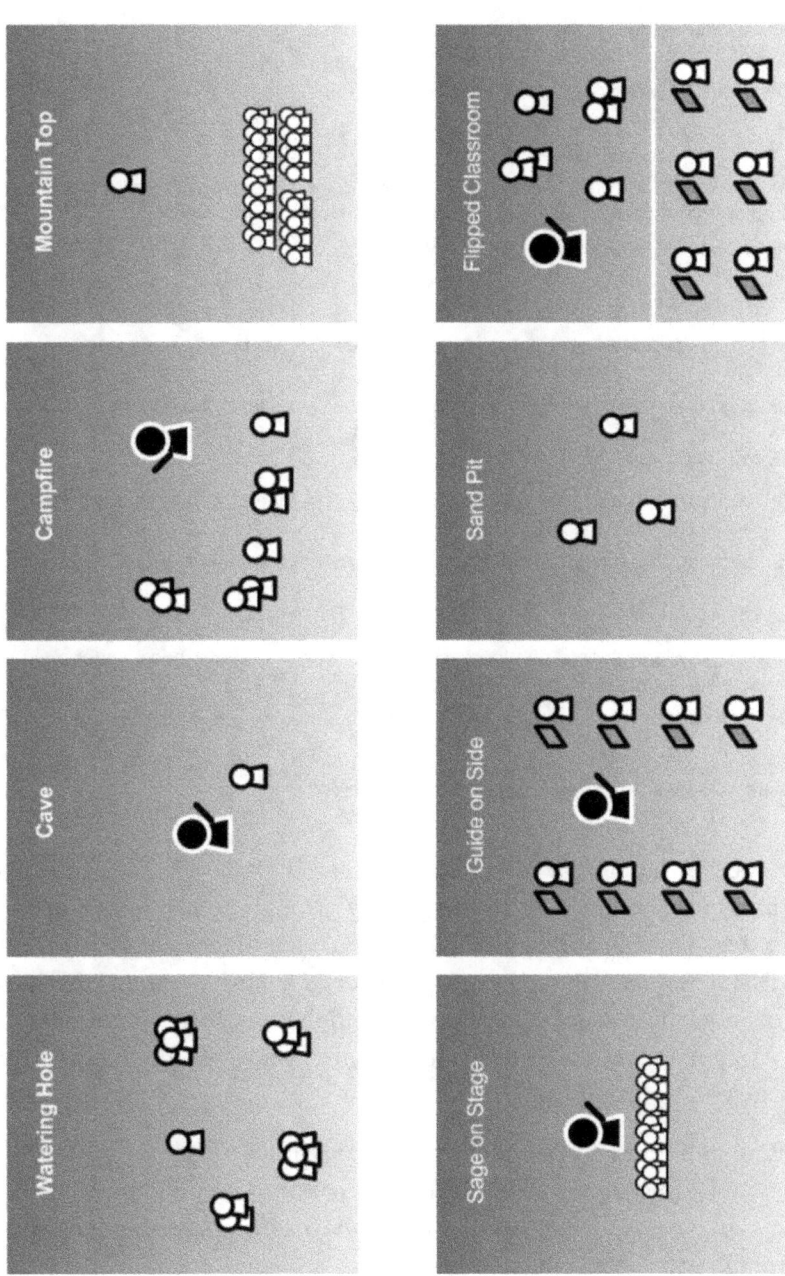

Figure 2.6

Watering Hole

Here you: come together to exchange ideas and cross-pollinate.

Think: a student learning programming and a student learning to dance sharing ideas about the creative process while having a drink.

Cave

Here you: withdraw from the noise of the classroom to be alone with your thoughts and reflection. A place to explore questions and make connections.

Think: a beanbag enclosed by bookshelves.

Campfire

Here you: share stories, exchange ideas and allow the group to build on each others' ideas.

Think: a group brainstorming ways to advertise their product to the community.

Mountain Top

Here you: celebrate and sharing your learning "one to many." You "sing it from the mountaintop."

Think: showing to the rest of your class a summary of your science project findings.

Sand Pit

Here you: play, prototype and experiment without worrying about mess, water or damaging surfaces.

Think: testing your bridge design to see if it can support the weight of a toy car.

Source: "Caves, Campfires, and Watering Holes," Core Education, http://www.core-ed.org/sites/events.core-ed.org/files/Caves-campfires-wateringholes.pdf

- Students taking classes in Active Learning Classrooms exceeded final grade expectations, suggesting strongly that features of the spaces contributed significantly to their learning.
- Different learning environments affect teaching-learning activities even when instructors attempt to hold these activities constant.
- Assignment types greatly impact the study environments that students select.[3]

What are the important points of this discussion?

David Thornburg describes different types of learning spaces in his book *Campfires in Cyberspace*, where he has brought these various "learning space" concepts to the forefront.

These models were also discussed in the 1990s and early twenty-first century. Pedagogically, the "sage on the stage" posited the benefit of the lecture, the professor who had knowledge to impart to the students. The "guide on the side" was a professor who "guided" students in their inquiry process, discovery, and development of a subject matter knowledge base.

Both of these models may be most applicable to the "campfire" learning space model, but they clearly differ in the instructor's approach to the students. All can be supported and enhanced using technology platforms.

Some classrooms, such as science classrooms with both a traditional classroom and wet lab environment, have been designed to support both models.

It could easily be argued that the "sage on the stage" model in the technology classroom would be when the students have their devices turned off and the instructor lectures.

However, the latest tablet and sharing software technologies can also allow the students to view the instructor's presentation and notes, and they can even live chat on their own devices during lecture.

Thus, the "guide on the side" model comes into play as the students perform activities on their devices while the instructor circulates and helps individual students and groups.

This is particularly relevant to the computer lab model in which rows of students use instructional or assessment applications with the instructor moving around overseeing progress.

This model also lends itself to a modified "watering hole" learning model where students work as small groups, either sharing a device or using their own, as the instructor oversees the small group work and provides guidance.

In these scenarios, the technology becomes the key to tracking progress and revisions, time and date stamping activities, recording the activities of participants (tracking which students are doing what work), and providing the sharing services that allow access to shared documents in real time for remote and asynchronous users.

Physical Spaces and Flexible Learning Spaces

The traditional bricks-and-mortar classroom is a box, mostly because it's the most efficient and effective way to divide the space in a building into multiple classrooms. The reason for a box-shaped classroom is similar to the reason a bubble is round (spherical). The box is based on physical and practical functionality and is not problematic on its own. The more important consideration is the use of the box.

There is a concept in school facilities program development of the "front of the classroom." This is a familiar concept that goes back to the days of the one-room schoolhouse and the chalkboard.

Having the teacher at the front of the classroom is so ingrained in programmatic design that many new schools and classrooms are built with "teaching walls" or "learning walls" where casework and cabinetry is built to facilitate the whiteboards and storage space for the teacher. The desks are oriented to "look" at the teaching wall, and the IWB or screens are mounted on or within these walls.

Flexible classrooms can be designed with wheeled furniture that can be easily arranged to form work groups or pods, and with collapsible tables for group work and computing in the rear of the classroom.

But once again, how are the teachers prepared to address the various layouts of the flexible classroom? When is there time to reorient the furniture? Where is the equipment mounted? What guidelines are provided to the architect during this design process?

Fortunately and unfortunately, unless you're building new schools (expanding enrollment or demolishing an old site), you may never have the opportunity to design new classrooms from scratch.

So where do you place the technology? It's fairly safe to say that if you're going to put up a projector and screen, or IWB, you're going to have to put it in the front of the classroom. It follows that the teacher's technology "suite" should be optimized for this application.

Consider having multiple displays in a classroom. Having three or four displays in each classroom would create more opportunity for students to share and make their work public. It would foster more collaboration and communication in your classrooms. All of these displays can be connected to a switching device that can display three or four screens. Or all screens can show the same display. This will help get away from the "teaching wall" model.

Teachers can also interact with their computer from a Bluetooth slate or tablet, which allows them to roam the classroom and not be dependent on a fixed location for providing instruction.

The use of a lectern or technology desk can also be debated endlessly. In primary grades, many teachers abhor the thought of a lectern, and many science classrooms have wet lab spaces that don't accommodate another lectern next to the island.

Should the teacher park a laptop next to the sink? If the teacher has a lectern in the front of the classroom, is there also a desk? Is the desk in front or in the rear of the classroom? Are the classrooms large enough to accommodate the teacher's desk in the rear and a lectern at the front?

Where's the phone? On the wall or on the teacher's desk? Where's the desk again?

We think each school or district should understand the concept of flexible space and possibly experiment with it—most likely in humanities classrooms, where less structured instructional models are appropriate.

This physical classroom is part of the physical layer of the EOSI model. As you analyze the physical classroom concept, the vision must acknowledge the limitations but maximize the opportunity for flexibility in the classroom. Then, technology can be implemented to enhance interactions between teachers and students.

Virtual Spaces

Classrooms and libraries can also become virtual spaces—that is, they can take on many models. Many new library or media center designs include flexible spaces, instructional spaces, and lab spaces, in addition to the typical carrels and bookshelves.

These spaces are to be shared by students and teachers, used by individuals and groups, and provide work space for projects. Some include broadcast studios with greenscreens and multimedia labs with high-end computers for graphic design and film editing.

These multiuse, multicapability facilities should be used to expand the vision and models for use beyond the classroom and individual students, impacting and interacting with the entire school and community as a whole. One example would be a public-use library that allows nonstudents access to library and computer lab facilities.

How do these learning space concepts fit into the vision?

Your vision must acknowledge the need for flexible learning spaces and virtual classrooms—not only physical spaces but also the various models of virtual spaces—as well as the ability to change or enhance the physical spaces to support the various learning space models.

How do the various learning spaces and teaching models support the curriculum? Or is the curriculum developed with specific learning spaces in mind?

Your vision must acknowledge the need to train teachers to use the learning space models—professional development must support the district's curriculum and classroom models.

Finally, do these models rise to the level of being included in your vision—or does your vision focus on one or two fundamental models?

NOTES

1. The first two definitions are from www.merriam-webster.com, the third is from www.dictionary.com, and the final definition is from Michael Porter, "What Is Strategy?," *Harvard Business Review,* November–December 1996.

2. Cynthia J. Brame, "Flipping the Classroom," Vanderbilt University Center for Teaching, accessed June 26, 2014, cft.vanderbilt.edu/guides-sub-pages/flipping-the-classroom/.

3. John S. Niles., *Transportation, Engineering and Planning – Vol. II – Telecommunications Substitutions for Transportation* (Seattle, WA: Global Telematics, 1992).

4. "Learning Spaces Research," IT@UMN, University of Minnesota, accessed June 26, 2014, it.umn.edu/services/all/academic-technology-support/research-evaluation/selected-research/learning-environments/.

CHAPTER 3

The Impact of Technology in Education

Before we dive into the technical realms, we provide a cautionary tale. You've heard it from us and many others before: any technology initiative is doomed to become a pet project if it cannot be standardized, replicated, trained, and implemented across the scope (whether the scope is a classroom, site, or district).

Just today I read a response from an educational technology website regarding using iPads in state testing:

> We just used about 400 iPads for testing on Friday. Overall, students were able to complete tests on them, but they were not without issues. Of all of our devices, iPads were the least liked by the students.
>
> We attached wired keyboards to them and the keyboard would sometimes drop off and need to be unplugged and plugged in again.
>
> The SecureTest app had issues and would sometimes just close down. Within the app, sometimes test questions would be greyed out, questions would not be answerable, students were unable to advance to the next screen, or the app would freeze.

Can you tell us again why they were using the iPads in the first place? Were they already owned by the school? Were they purchased for the testing? If the testing or curriculum was really the objective, why were iPads chosen? With this type of review, will the school continue buying iPads?

Following is a deep dive into the fundamental building blocks of technology use within education. They are as follows:

- Precepts for student learning
- Effective use of technology
- Technology platforms
  - Education technology platforms
  - Data integration platforms
  - Information technology platforms
  - Infrastructure
  - Support and sustainability

It may seem overwhelming at first. But, as we wend our way through each of the following sections, keep in mind that we are trying to see the future! The visionaries in your organization along with the educators and the technologists must work together to create the vision. It cannot be done in a vacuum by one individual. Just remember: focus on the curriculum.

PRECEPTS FOR STUDENT LEARNING

The vision should encompass fundamental precepts or goals for guiding student learning and should have a fundamental emphasis on Common Core precepts. These precepts are the ideas to relate to students as the cornerstone of their learning. Each precept may be enhanced and augmented using technology. In fact, some of the precepts, such as digital citizenship, exist only because of technology.

Examples of these precepts may include the following:

- Collaboration—working cooperatively
- Communication
- Critical thinking
- Creativity
- Acting ethically, including digital citizenship
- Learning to learn
- Lifelong learning

Once again, Bloom's taxonomy may provide some of the precepts (the higher levels, of course), while other precepts might be specific to the focus of your school or district.

For instance, the vision of a performing arts magnet school might include a precept focused on the arts and related skills, and the vision of a STEM academy might include a science or engineering emphasis.

Each stakeholder should be able to understand the influence their involvement with the learning process may have on students.

For instance, do faculty members practice and encourage lifelong learning by adopting new tools to enhance student's learning experience, instead of sticking to the same old PowerPoint slides?

Do administrators model digital citizenship by interacting in the district chat board and responding directly to letters from parents?

How do learning precepts fit into or support the vision?

How are precepts communicated and supported through professional development?

EFFECTIVE USE OF TECHNOLOGY

Every district is tasked with the development of a technology plan. As a consultant for strategic planning, I might ask whether the technology plan aligns with the district's strategic plan. The technology plan can align with the strategic plan only if the strategic plan is developed first, with technology as a key consideration.

Envision a technology plan that states, "By 2014, 30 percent of teachers will use a learning management system." It would be logical to ask whether there is a district-wide learning management system and whether there is a district-wide license (or at least a license for 30 percent of the students).

The technology plan cannot be a silo—it cannot only have a vertical impact within the organization. Rather, the technology plan must be fully embedded within the core of the strategic plan. Thus, the technology plan can become a true implementation plan that includes actual designs, budgets, and implementation timelines.

At this point it might be logical to ask how technology applies to a vision. Isn't the vision unaffected by technology? The answer is yes, inasmuch as the vision is not dependent on technology. But it is well within the relevant scope to embed the use of technology into the vision to insure a process of inquiry that relies on bringing forth the efficiencies, features, and functions of new technologies, as these examples indicate:

- A vision that includes mobility within the learning environment becomes dependent on a wireless infrastructure.
- A vision of students working on projects in small groups is enabled by a collaboration suite of software.
- A vision of standardized curriculum and professional development is enhanced by a learning management system.

How does the effective use of technology support the vision?

How does the vision reflect the effective use of technology?

Until this point, we've tried to stay above the technical details. Our first encounter with technology is in the following context—SAMR: Substitution, Augmentation, Modification, Redefinition.

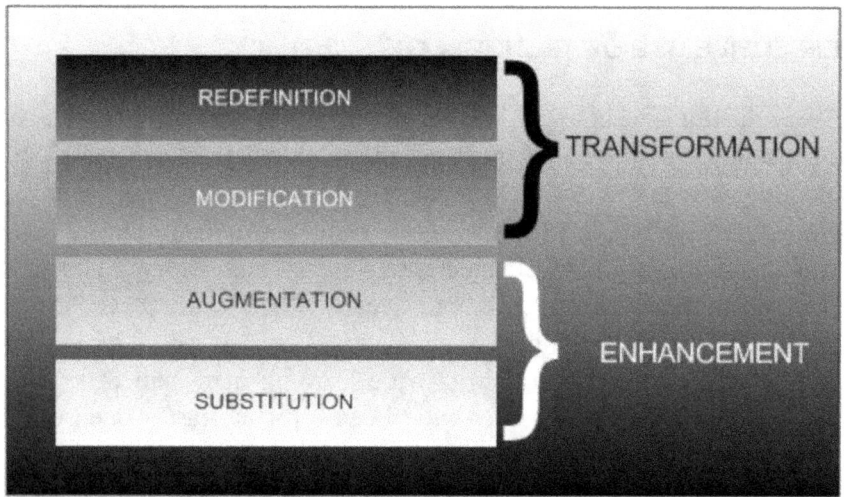

Figure 3.1 Ruben R. Puentedura, PhD, defines these levels of technology integration.

ENHANCING CURRICULUM USING TECHNOLOGY

In the early days of classroom technology integration we saw the introduction of presentation enhancement technologies, such as the following:

- Overhead projector
- Filmstrips

- Projector and screen (to display computer graphics)
- PowerPoint
- Document camera
- Interactive whiteboards

These technologies and the way they have been used have been little more than the lower levels of the SAMR model—enhancement of communication.

How many times have you walked into a classroom to see a teacher writing on a piece of paper below a document camera?

Here are technology components (screen, projector, cabling, computer, document camera, plus other tech frills) that cost more than $10,000 being used in the same way as an overhead projector aimed at the wall.

PowerPoint presentations—or, as we refer to it, "death by PowerPoint"—may be the most widely practiced example of misuse of technology, but such misuse is entirely dependent on the content and delivery of the material.

A simple bulleted PowerPoint slide can be enhanced in a multitude of ways, such as by adding audio and video clips, experiments, and a variety of student engagement exercises.

So, once again, we're talking about execution and professional development. And all the same lessons were true twenty years ago before the digital classroom.

By using the SAMR model to examine current technology use, you may find that your investment in technology is either not producing the change in instructional practice or that professional development is not providing the impetus to move up the model. This simple assessment should help you determine the impact of your technology program: Are we just doing the same thing in a new way? Or are we doing something new and creative that we never really could do before? Are we thinking 10×?

Google Apps for Education (GAFE) is an excellent example of a technology that redefines word processing. Students can use it to do more than enter, edit, and format text on a page: it allows students and teachers to comment, share documents, collaborate, and communicate their writing. It is truly transformational as a technology tool.

It's also extremely cost-effective—it's *free* and requires virtually no support from your information technology department. Google Apps for Education is accessible from any device with a web browser.

But don't take it for granted that the feature set alone will cause the transformation—you can bet that GAFE can also be used as "just a word processor" if that is all the teacher or program requires. Once again, professional development is key to transforming instruction in a classroom and will dictate the site-wide or district-wide impact.

Focus your professional development on the integration of technology, not on devices.

CHAPTER 4

Technology Platforms

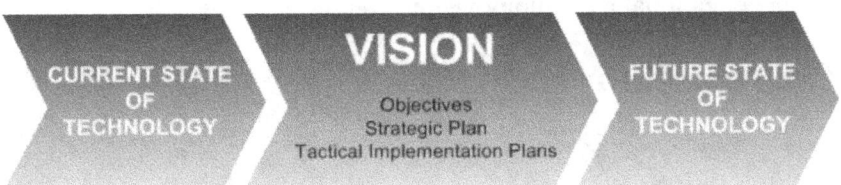

Figure 4.1

The educational technology vision is a product of the need to move from a current state to a defined future state. The process of defining the current state requires discovery and inquiry. The process of defining the future state requires a similar inquiry, but based on curricular goals and objectives. And, finally, the gap analysis will define the strategy and tactics required to move from the current state to the future defined state.

What does that all mean? It's the butterfly effect in practice: the finer details ultimately define the scope of the vision. In turn, the vision helps all participants and stakeholders understand the objectives, strategy, tactics, tasks, and activities.

In this section we'll discuss technology platforms, and as in much of our technical analysis, we use the EOSI model to analyze these platforms. But before we delve into the technical depth of these platforms, it is once again important to ask the question, how do these technical details affect the overall vision?

The greatest thinkers and visionaries see the future through the prism of their experience and knowledge base.

40 CHAPTER 4

Physicists foresee vast and powerful microprocessor technologies that enable mindboggling computing power and capability.

Biologists and geneticists envision breakthroughs in medicine and genetics, while engineers and architects envision innovative living and learning spaces.

They can envision and even predict the future because of their underlying understanding of the fundamental building blocks of their science. Similarly, an educational technology vision requires an understanding of the current state of technologies and practices and the fundamentals of education, delivery, and assessment. The technologies that can aid and enhance these fundamental activities become the building blocks for an educational technology vision.

EOSI TECHNOLOGY PLATFORMS

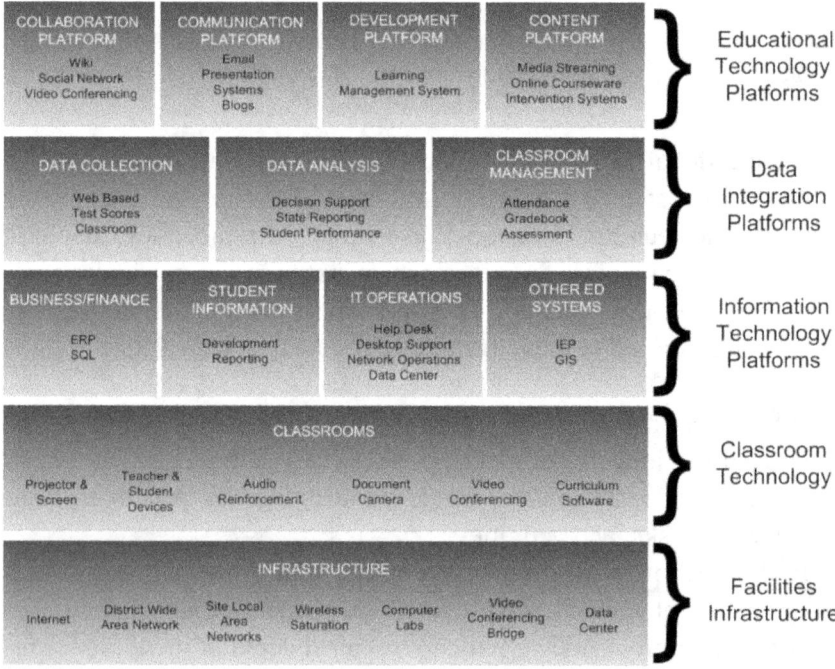

Figure 4.2

At the top of the stack are the educational technology platforms. These are the applications (software and systems) that directly support the classroom and instruction. This is not the curriculum but the tools that support curriculum.

Two levels below are the information technology (IT) platforms. These applications support the business of running a school district: financials, student information, operations management, transportation, and so forth.

Between these layers are the data integration platforms. Applications at this layer provide the connection—or integration—between the district business systems and the classroom instructional systems. For instance, the gradebook module (data integration layer) is the conduit between the educational technology platform layer (entering student grades) and the student information system (SIS) at the information technology platform layer.

As we move down the EOSI technology platforms and discuss them, you may wonder how these lower-level details affect the vision. Well, they don't—and they do!

Developing a fundamental understanding of these building blocks is a necessary exercise.

One of the initial tasks in creating a vision and strategic plan is getting a clear understanding of the current state of the "things" and the technology infrastructure.

EDUCATIONAL TECHNOLOGY PLATFORMS

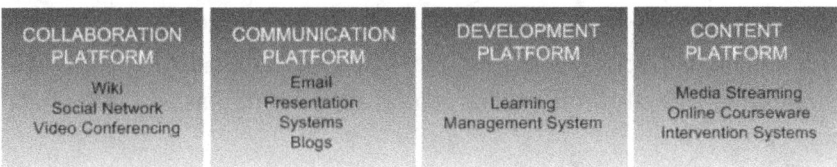

Figure 4.3

The education technology platforms defined above are the fundamental systems that support the curriculum and classroom instruction. Notice that although each system supports classroom instruction, the systems are hosted and supported by the IT infrastructure (servers in the data center) and the IT department.

Collaboration

Collaboration systems are the sharing and networking applications that allow students to work with each other, share ideas and notes, and collaborate on projects and homework. Applications that support collaborative work and sharing such as wikis, Edmodo, and VoiceThread are common examples in education.

Communication

Communication systems support two types of communication—messaging between users and presentation to users. This includes the electronic mail system and software such as Prezi or even PowerPoint that enhances a user's ability to communicate to others.

Development

These next two platforms—development and content—can become the fundamental building blocks of a school or district's curriculum. These are the areas where the district must make a commitment in investment and professional development.

The development platform is the system selected to create content. Teachers and the curriculum department must be provided with tools, templates, and standardized methods to create, develop, and ultimately share their lesson plans.

The development platform might be as simple as using GAFE, Word, Excel, and PowerPoint for curriculum development. The curriculum department might provide standard templates, themes, and guidelines that allow all teachers to create content that is standardized and consistent.

The professional development department must define the approach and standards to communicate to all teachers and support their development endeavors.

Of course, many sophisticated content development systems are available and expensive, requiring major IT infrastructure, software licensing, and professional development.

Some of these systems are so complex that teachers never begin to use all the functions and features.

Content

The content system is where all this standardized curriculum lives. You can imagine that if every teacher is creating standardized content that can be shared, then a system must be implemented to catalog and manage all that content. Yes, it's a big server and a lot of storage, but, beyond that, it is a platform for managing, sharing, and streaming content to classrooms and devices.

Imagine a school's private YouTube, where all the science experiments and historical reenactments are at your fingertips for lessons and sharing. You can see how this system could be the key to flipping the classroom.

Many districts have not made the commitment or investment in a standardized content platform. Teachers are free to develop their own content, but when it comes to sharing, other nondistrict resources come into play, such as the lesson plan libraries of Smart's Notebook software or Promethean Planet.

These are vast stores of shared content and lesson plans, but the district or school has no control of, management over, or filter on these lesson plans. How can a district implement standardized templates or formats for lesson plans when the teachers are free to go to these warehouses and download someone else's lessons?

DATA INTEGRATION PLATFORMS

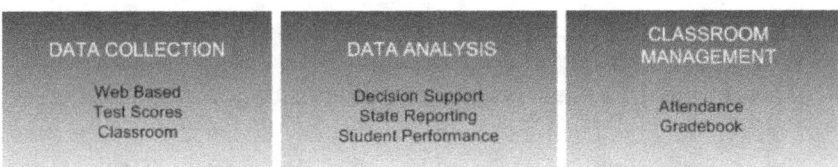

Figure 4.4

Data integration platforms lie between the educational technology platforms described above and the information technology platforms below.

These platforms may be modules of an IT platform, such as an attendance or gradebook application that is part of an SIS, or individual applications that are designed to provide integration between the classroom and the IT system. A stand-alone decision support system that harvests data from the SIS and provides summary data to administrators is an example.

This is an important layer because all schools have the lower-level information technology platforms (in some form and function) and most schools have instructional applications and classroom software, but the integration platforms extend the data in the IT platforms, making them functional and generating reports that can be used to leverage information in the classroom and elsewhere—for instance, state reporting.

Once again, this data integration platform impacts vision through expansion of the role of data, through expansion of the data collected, reported, and referenced.

Data Collection

Data are often collected at this layer through a database application that compiles data that may not exist within the realm of the SIS. Applications such as specific testing requirements or decision support systems provide access to new data types that may not exist within the lower level IT systems.

This becomes a major responsibility for the information technology and educational services departments because once data is created and then reported, it becomes historical and then must be verifiable (data integrity) and maintained (database administration).

Thus the act of collecting data can and will become a "system" in and of itself, and will need resources, policies, and procedures to be maintained.

Think of the time that someone compiled data from "this report and that report" and made an Excel spreadsheet. This happens all the time, in every organization. *However*, how did the creator of this report validate the data used? Were the calculations done correctly? And, more importantly, once this report is published and requested—say monthly—whose responsibility is it to maintain this manually created report?

So, the salient point of this component of the data integration layer is that data collection must occur using systems where data integrity is verified and reporting is automated.

Data Analysis

Data analysis is the specific reporting for decision support. The data analysis allow users of this new data to massage and manipulate the reporting formats in order to better understand the data collected and to make important instructional decisions based on this data.

The data analysis tools allow the user to perform "what-if" scenarios, to understand cause and effect if specific factors in the reporting process are changed.

Once again, the idea is to support various departments, users, and stakeholders with verified and automatic information that did not exist before the collection, compilation, and reporting of this "new" data.

The most effective application of this impacts assessment and evaluation. Whereas the typical student information system may contain or help you collect and store certain types of data, analysis tools are usually not built into the system's software.

The vision needs incorporate the understanding that the data is compiled and utilized to add value to the instructional decision-making process.

Data to Inform Instruction

School districts often describe the need to use data to inform instruction. The tricky part of this is being able to answer the related questions: What data is needed? How is it collected? Where will it be stored? How is it accessed?

Schools typically want to use as many different data points as they can to get the whole picture of what a child knows or doesn't know. The data could be objective or subjective, formative or substantive in nature.

Using data to inform instruction is not a simple process for teachers to tackle. Teachers want easy-to-use reports that they can run. Teachers are trained neither in the art of data manipulation nor in how to write reports or extracts to get to the data they need.

Using data to inform instruction is a *commitment of resources* that a district must make in order to be successful. The following are some of the considerations:

- Defining source data: What is the source data, and what format is it in?
- Where is the source data physically located?
- How is the data accessed?
- Will a data warehouse be created to store disparate data? The data need to be in a single system or set of reporting tables that allows users to create meaningful queries (and allows teachers to generate reports).
- Is the user interface friendly and easy to use?
- What training will teachers receive on how to read and use information they get in a report?
- What process will be used to create new reports?

If your organization doesn't already have a database administrator (DBA) on staff and a resource at the district level to help teachers understand and use the data, additional staff and resources will be necessary. These resources should be able to "translate" what the teachers are asking for in the form of reports and communicate that effectively to your DBA. The teachers shouldn't have to know how to create reports from data—they should be spending their time on interpreting data and using it to help inform instruction.

Before diving headfirst into this endeavor, beware of the most common pitfalls, some of which we've already discussed and others we'll mention later. The most basic ones are these:

- Using off-the-shelf reports that aren't valuable to the user
- Selecting inaccurate data (searches and sorts that aren't specific to that user that may skew the report, such as when a teacher creates a report and mistakenly includes or excludes data in the search and sort process)
- Not understanding the intent of a specific report

The important points are to determine the data required for the specific user (teacher or administrator; student, class, or school), and to commit the resources to develop the report(s). Then, test the report across multiple users and validate the accuracy of the data selection and the actual data (sometimes the actual data are garbage—such as when users enter data into fields for their own use or when users utilize nonstandard abbreviations or data entries that cause search and sort errors).

Different users will require different reports. Teachers need reports specific to their classes and student bases that can be compared to other classes at similar grade levels—at their school, other district schools, and even other schools at a state or national level.

Similarly, administrators require data and reports for their collective classes, teachers, disciplines, and schools and will value comparable data from other district schools and other schools outside the district as well.

Oftentimes, the off-the-shelf reports are adequate, but the real value comes when the user truly understands the meaning and purpose of the data and can make day-to-day decisions in the classroom based on the data.

Classroom Management

Gradebook and attendance applications are likely the most common classroom management modules offered by major SISs. These are examples of using legacy SIS data to make the classroom experience more efficient for the teacher.

The visionary point to these classroom modules is that technology and data are "leveraged"—meaning more benefit is exploited from the legacy and integration layer databases than the legacy or new data offers as a stand-alone data island.

INFORMATION TECHNOLOGY PLATFORMS

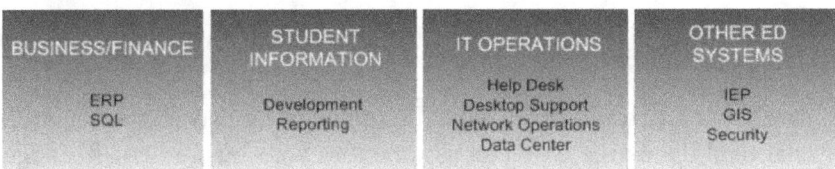

Figure 4.5

The information technology platforms are the traditional data processing systems that have been around forever to run the business of a school system. Fortunately, for the purposes of this book we don't need to tell you what you already know, so we'll just include some not-so-obvious commentary.

We struggled with how to address these areas for this book—it's kind of like writing about plumbing in an architectural design book. But the analogy holds, if taken from the performance requirements point of view: the architectural guide would include the details so that all basic necessities of plumbing—water supply, drainage, bath and shower facilities, mechanical systems (HVAC), fire suppression, kitchen, landscape, and irrigation needs—are addressed. But your particular architectural guide may include plumbing for interior waterscapes and landscaping, pools, drinking fountains, exterior waterfalls, and conveyances—maybe you need a moat!

Another thought about these IT systems is that they are a necessary evil—you can't run your business without one. Unfortunately, some small school districts and even some medium-size ones, for whatever reason, have no authority or control over their business or financial enterprise resource planning system (if it is an ERP).

They may be using a county- or state-based payroll and financial system and aren't large enough to warrant bringing it in-house.

To complicate this, cloud-based financial and student information systems make the traditional cost comparisons very difficult at best.

How do you compare a cloud-based ERP service to the current county-based legacy payroll system you've been using since we were all born? How do you quantify the fact that new report formats and data types cannot be added to the legacy systems?

The salient point is that these fundamental business systems must fulfill the following performance requirements.

Relational Database

If you've heard someone in your IT organization say, "It's not even a relational database," you can assume that your business or financial system is antiquated.

That's not to say that you can't continue to run your operation on this system, only that enhancements and integration with other value-added applications may be limited—particularly at the data integration layer.

Microsoft SQL Server and Oracle are the relational database platforms for almost every ERP on the market today.

There are still many COBOL-based financial systems out there still running, and they will continue to run until the hardware fails or the COBOL programmer retires—then you'll find your organization in a real pickle.

The important fact is that all new systems, even cloud-based systems, are developed on a relational database system, which is optimal for many technical reasons, not the least of which is the ability to find database administrators, programmers, and developers who can work on these platforms.

Customizable

Business systems platforms and applications must be customizable. No two districts are the same, and thus no two operate the same. The more flexible your business system (which also alludes to the need for programmers and developers), the more it can change as the organization changes the way it does business.

The less customizable a business system is, the more it will be customized in an inappropriate manner. For instance, think of the column 6 that someone decided to use to track second emergency numbers because it wasn't already in the system.

That field may not be numerically constrained, and thus someone could type letters in the field when it should be numbers only. Then how do you get that column 6 secondary emergency number to show up in a report?

Similarly, the more your organization customizes its business system, the less able the vendor will be to support it. Conversely, the more your vendor customizes your business system for you, the more dependent your organization becomes on them for further modifications and support—sounds fun!

End-User Reporting Function

The IT department must be able to provide full reporting functionality—if the data is in there, there must be a way to get it out, format it, validate it, and then automate the function. If the analysts can't do this, your financial system may be limiting the level of data integration that can happen at your district or school.

For instance, if you can't collect and report the new data types needed by the latest state reporting requirements within your current system, then you must develop an additional data collection and management functionality (read new database) that allows you to collect it, format it, validate it, and automate it, *then* connect it with the source financial and/or student data.

Don't even try to use Excel for a task like this. If you do, the only assurance you will have is that the data integrity is in question, and the manual creation of this report just became someone's job task.

Service Level Agreements

You've heard of being held hostage by the programmers—that's when your department and its reporting capabilities are totally controlled by the whims, wishes, and availability of your vendor.

The only way to manage these relationships and mitigate disputes is with contracted service level agreements (SLAs).

The SLAs should provide request processes, response times, and a specific development and quality assurance (QA) process that dictates the methods and expectations for communications and interactions between your organization and your vendor. Liquidated damages can be detailed and triggered based on agreed-upon baselines and metrics. Without these contracted items, your department is available to be taken hostage.

Quality Assurance

This area is always ignored until you've published a report with incorrect data. Then all the questions that should have been asked and verified before publication come up:

- Where did the data come from?
- Where did the calculations come from?
- Who validated it?

- Who approved it?
- Was it tested?

There's only one way to avoid these types of questions. It is well defined in IT infrastructure library (ITIL) change management, but it ends like this: test, test, test.

Your vendor must have a test environment that mimics your internal environment and provides them the comprehensive ability to test and validate new functions and reports before ever being introduced to the production environment and real data.

Quality assurance procedures must be in place for all external and internal development and reporting.

INFORMATION TECHNOLOGY OPERATIONS

You might not have considered this, but your IT operation has become the lifeblood of the organization. And, much like health care, your organization either prioritizes IT operations near the top, like a health nut, or the near the bottom, like a drug addict.

The health nut is proactive about his health, eats well, monitors his blood pressure, exercises, gets regular physicals, and avoids fatty foods.

The drug addict drinks too much, stays up late, eats whatever, injects poisons into his blood, and only changes his behavior in response to medical emergencies.

If your IT operations department doesn't operate like the health nut—planning upgrades, monitoring performance, managing traffic loads—then your organization will eventually suffer like a drug addict—responding to life-threatening ailments just in time to stay alive, never really getting out of danger, never gaining ground for better health and a brighter future.

The IT operation must implement industry-standard practices and tools to be like the health nut. These practices are well detailed in the information technology infrastructure library (ITIL).

Unfortunately, the applicable documents, processes, and procedures are focused on large organizations and complex IT environments.

However, even the smallest IT operations department can benefit from implementing policies and procedures detailed in ITIL. The information technology service management (ITSM) system is a workflow system that helps an IT organization manage the operations of the IT department.

With the explosion of devices coming to a school site near you (think BYOD and 1:1), this is like the drug addict getting too much heroin. One small dose is one thing, but when injected in amounts ten to one hundred times that dose, the result is death. Similarly, if your current network barely supports its current device count (you can tell this by perceived performance of your computing and Internet access), then when you introduce one hundred times the number of devices, you can be sure it will just collapse.

An enterprise ITSM should minimally encompass two broad scopes of IT operations: problem management and change management.

Problem Management

Problem management is the process and act of tracking, detailing, resolving, and cataloging IT problems. Every ITSM operation must use some sort of call tracking and problem management mechanism, or the organization will be in chaos—reacting to the squeakiest wheel (the loudest or most important user) and unable to accurately monitor and report resolutions and overall activity.

It can be as simple as a spreadsheet, where the help desk analyst records the issue and user, assigns a tracking number, and begins the process of troubleshooting and resolution.

With no comprehensive ITSM system for problem management, the IT department is unable to do the following:

- Track and age calls
- Assign calls according to call load and/or expertise
- Track escalation of calls
- Track call resolution and time
- Compile call resolutions (knowledge base)
- Set baseline call metrics
- Set call metric improvement goals

- Analyze call load and type (problem distribution)
- Analyze problem trends (trend analysis)
- Plan mitigation initiatives (training)
- Track resources (FTE justification)

The best way to illustrate this need is by asking your IT director the following questions about the help desk and IT support organization:

- What is the department's average call resolution time?
- What is the average monthly call load for each resource?

If your IT director cannot answer these questions, then how could they possibly make the assertion (assuming you've heard this in your organization) that they're understaffed. When encountering a comment like this, I typically respond with one of the above questions. Not only are these metrics a measurement of efficacy of your department and its resources, but they are also the baseline for improvement. And if the IT department has no baseline metric for improvement, all their efforts and activities are *reactive*.

This also means that if they are improving (or the opposite—getting worse), there's no measurement or basis for that conclusion either. This is not to say that an IT department cannot run without an ITSM problem management system; it certainly can, but chaos will reign as the department is driven by emergencies and prioritized by squeaky wheels.

Change Management

Change management is an equally important function of the ITSM system but usually tackled as second priority—and that's OK, as long as it is addressed.

Change management is the proactive part of the ITSM operation, while problem management is the reactive part. In bigger organizations a project management office (PMO) may be in charge of change management. But the point is that nothing in the enterprise can just be changed without user, system, network, and nontechnical impacts, so change management processes must be in place.

Further, the most significant activity in change management is nontechnical—it's *communication*. This is where unexpected catastrophic chains of events are to be mitigated. For instance, your network engineer says, "We need to upgrade the routing firmware per the manufacturer— it'll take about five minutes. We'll do it during lunch." Then the whole network crashes because *all* of the switches will also need to be upgraded.

Or when one of your computer lab teachers adds an unmanaged minihub to the network and accidentally creates a loop and crashes the site network. In these instances, a simple e-mail between the end-user, in this case, the computer lab teacher, and IT should trigger change management procedures and mitigate network and user downtime.

The most common change management activity is the MAC (move, add, and change), and the MAC impacts many departments, not just IT. So the change management process may be administered by the ITSM, but all departments must use the process.

When a move is scheduled, the change management system will initiate a workflow such as this: facilities move request, voice move request, equipment move request, networking, wireless, credentials, security, signage, and so on.

But the most salient point of this discussion is that the ITSM policies and procedures are *practices* supported by *systems*.

Just because the systems are in place does not mean that the individuals will follow the practices and procedures. Practices must be communicated, advocated, and enforced by leadership and the directors. The practices must be ingrained throughout the organization.

What good is the help desk system if the superintendent's administrative assistant calls the IT director when there is an issue? Or if the facilities director plans a move but doesn't inform the IT department (and new switches need to be installed before the move can begin)?

Data derived from problem management may trigger change management. For instance, if the problem distribution report shows that a software update is required, then a change management process may be triggered to plan a software upgrade distribution. This change will likely trigger a test lab, procurement of software and licenses, a schedule of upgrades, a rollout plan, communication to departments, scheduled downtime, deployment, and follow-up support and reporting. It *never* just takes five minutes!

Network Operations Center (NOC)

Through this discussion you may begin to recognize that the district network carries the lifeblood of district operations *and* instruction. Yes, face it. Everything has become dependent on the WiFi, LAN (local area network), WAN (wide area network), and Internet connectivity—and that is just the plumbing. Don't make me list the one hundred other things your ITSM, IT department, and surrounding resources must also support.

To complicate things, the instructional initiatives will promulgate numerous and new devices: 1:1, BYOD, and all the other technology initiatives you can list.

The NOC then becomes the heart monitor of your organization. If you have to ask your IT director if you have a NOC, then you probably don't have one. But that doesn't mean you can't implement a NOC. A NOC is simply a suite of monitoring and alarm tools that provide proactive monitoring of the network's utilization and performance along with defined processes and procedures.

A real enterprise NOC will also be tightly integrated with the ITSM so that events may trigger problem management and/or change management processes. For instance (and this example will affect everyone reading this), the proliferation of end-user devices using the network may cause the network monitoring software to spike to 90 percent at peak traffic times, which will in turn trigger a 10Gbps backbone upgrade at each school site. Shall we run the budget numbers for this upgrade?

Data Center/Cloud

At a recent presentation, I was talking about data center virtualization and the centralization of compute and storage resources when one IT director said, "We're moving everything to the cloud, no district data center."

The reasons for and against these architectures are way, way beyond the scope and scale of this book. In fact, even the definitions of these two architectures are more than may need to be understood relative to technology vision.

The data center concept is self-descriptive. Implementing a data center means moving all compute and storage resources to the center of the district, in a protected and environmentally controlled area. The data center should have redundant power, telecom service, and cooling—Tier 2 or Tier 3. Assets are capitalized and depreciated. All systems are "on-prem" and owned by the district. Yes, it's costly, but it is more efficient and manageable than the distributed alternative (think, servers at every school in uncooled MDF [Main Distributing Framework, aka telephone closets] rooms). Success is measured by the ongoing operations of each system and hopefully the ITSM reporting metrics.

The cloud concept is a pure outsourced option. All compute and storage resources are "off-prem." None of the hardware, software, or facilities are capitalized. The premise is that the service provider is offering Tier 3 or Tier 4 facilities redundancy, a level beyond what an individual district could build.

Success is attained through service level agreements and maintenance contracts. You will integrate your ITSM system with theirs or maybe use theirs exclusively.

Unfortunately, this complex philosophical decision will rest mostly on your legacy architecture and hopefully be driven by curricular goals.

We hate to leave this issue sitting unresolved, but we may have reached a level of granularity beyond a vision development book. The good news is that these architectures are not necessarily exclusive. That is, your district may implement a hybrid of data center and cloud-based applications, or, rather, your district *will* implement a hybrid of these because, for some applications, it will be unavoidable.

So there, we've let ourselves off the hook.

Security

Security may be the most expansive and expensive initiative, outside of facilities, that a school or district could undertake. With the recent school shootings burned into our memories and a slew of small, easy-to-steal technology devices proliferating like wildfire, the many varieties and flavors of security, property protection, and safety cannot be ignored.

Here's an abridged list of items related to security, emergency, and safety that warrant some consideration in the educational technology vision development process:

Physical Security

- Video surveillance
  - Property protection is addressed by using fixed cameras and a video management systems (VMS) to record and archive video footage for later reference.
  - Safety efforts use active monitoring (security personnel) and/or analytics-based monitoring to provide alerts in the case of defined security or safety-related activities.
- Access control
  - "Key cards," RFID, and "proximity cards" can be used to control access to campus ingress/egress, building ingress/egress, and/or classroom ingress/egress. Access can be scheduled, audit tracked, and alert monitored.
- Intrusion detection
  - Hard contacts, infrared sensors, and motion sensors can be used to trigger alarms.

The most important technical factor in today's security context is that it should *all* be IP based. That means it all should be on your network. And it means that all the bandwidth provisioning your IT department just did for the 1:1 and BYOD initiatives probably did not include the addition of as many as fifty to one hundred IP-based cameras on each site.

I once developed a long-range master technology plan for a large district, and after presenting a multimillion-dollar budget to upgrade the core switches in every school to 1Gbps (it was in the early 2000s), the director asked about the budget for IP-based video security. He almost kicked me out of his office when I said, "Double it."

Network Security

- Internet
  - Outbound web filter
  - Mail filter

- Fire walls
- Virus filter
- Access Control Lists (ACL)
- Virtual Local Area Networks (VLANs)
- DMZs
* Wireless Security
  - Access server
  - Encryption

Emergency Communications

* Outbound communications (reverse 911)
* Enhanced 911
* Emergency operations center.

Here's one way to look at it: if the vision that emerges from your development process includes the words "safe" or "safety" or "security," your vision must encompass all the above areas.

CHAPTER 5

Classrooms

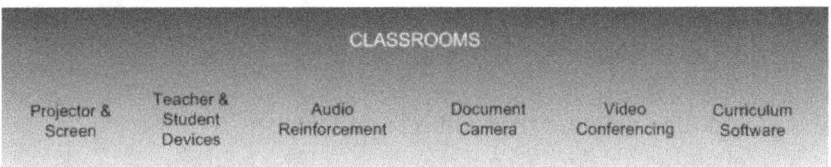

Figure 5.1

As we discuss the classroom and related technology, it becomes important to understand that the systems and technologies encompassed in the vision for the classroom cost a lot of money.

This is not necessarily because they are that expensive but rather because each classroom will require the same (or similar) technology. As you consider the tools, devices, software, and support, you will quickly see the need to constrain the scope and scale of the actual implementation.

Although the vision is far-reaching, the actual implementation is often for a much smaller group and over a longer time period.

For instance, when your district did its most recent wireless upgrade, were they able to provide wireless saturation to all classrooms? Or was the implementation limited to a certain few sites or buildings?

You can experiment by building a bill of materials (BOM) for equipment that should go into every classroom, then multiply by the number of classrooms. Before you get up off the ground, let me warn you that the result is probably less than half the dollars necessary to really implement the classroom technology.

Why? That's in the next section. First let's consider the following:

TEACHER TOOLS

We think we can all agree that every teacher needs a device, either a laptop or desktop, of greater performance and functionality than a standard student computer. It should be robust enough to handle the delivery and presentation of all streaming and local data types, as well as be able to run all the teacher's administrative and development apps using rich media types.

Teachers should have access to a standard suite of productivity, classroom management, learning management system (LMS), communications (e-mail), and collaboration tools (GAFE).

But does the teacher need the following?:

- a desktop computer (in addition to a laptop)
- a tablet (or a device to remotely control the laptop)
- a phone or intercom system
- voice or sound amplification (think about every teacher)
- assisted listening
- document camera
- cable television
- lectern or technology desk
- method to record and take a picture of the classroom
- video conferencing
- professional development and coaching

STUDENT TOOLS

Here's what we've witnessed in the last twenty years for students.

- Apple II labs and PC labs (1980s)
- Mac and PC labs (1990s)
- Student laptops (early 2000s)
- Apple iPods and student laptops (2002–2005)
- Clicker devices, student interactive remotes, iPods, and netbooks (2005–2010)

- Apple iPads and netbooks (2010)
- Android tablets, Windows 8 tablets, Apple iPads, smartphones, and Chromebooks (2011–present)

Based on the amount of time required for each of these platforms to proliferate and then become obsolete, we can only assume that some kind of BYOD, 1:1, and Common Core hybrid initiative will require that everyone has something, with a minimum screen size and resolution, wireless networking, and browser compatibility. Beyond that, all bets are off. How'd you like to be the developer and patent holder of the infrared voting remote that came and left the market faster than POGS? (Remember the milk caps that were a popular game and trading cap in the 1990s?)

BRING YOUR OWN DEVICE: IT'S NOT A QUESTION OF STRATEGY ANYMORE

I know you're asking how it's not a strategy when you haven't even formulated your strategy yet. It is on your to do list, right?

Bring Your Own Device is your current reality. It's an unfunded mandate for each IT department. Like it or not, they're on your premises. They may not access your network, but they'll be walking around your campus whether you like it or not. Unfortunately, if you haven't addressed guest access, outbound filtering, and internal wireless security networks (VLANs), then those devices are already flying around unsecured and tying up your WiFi.

Once you decide what your district policy will be and get it approved by the board, then you can go get the dollars and deal with all the security, filtering, and access control appliances. Soon, right? As with all district-wide technology components, you will have to build in redundancy as well.

The question then becomes whether BYOD is part of your *curriculum* strategy. Not necessarily. Once you realize that your network use policy and your curriculum strategy are somewhat independent of each other, it will be much easier to do the necessary planning.

Consider BYOD in two separate contexts: infrastructure and curriculum.

In the BYOD infrastructure architecture we allow users to connect to our network and services, and filter and constrain access to resources based on their devices and usernames.

In the BYOD curriculum architecture, the assumption is that a certain web-based application compatible with most mobile devices would be chosen by a school, grade, or class. Students (and teachers) may choose to access the application using their own device or a school device.

Note that in the BYOD curriculum context, there must also be some sort of 1:1 or district-provided device if some students don't have their own devices.

BYOD OR 1:1

Many districts seem to be pondering questions surrounding BYOD and 1:1. In fact, LinkedIn has at least one group dedicated to K-12 BYOD, and many other groups are discussing it. One primary discussion thread is specifically about BYOD versus 1:1.

We believe, however, that this inquiry is flawed. Comparing the two is like comparing apples and oranges—or, dare I say it, Macs and PCs. As we stated above, BYOD in its native form is an infrastructure requirement, not a curricular initiative; it is a question of policy (wireless and security).

One-to-one, on the other hand, is a curricular initiative. The 1:1 requirement must be based on curricula that require each student to have a device. This inquiry will also help determine the type of student device.

When you see a district debating hardware platforms for 1:1, you might bet that the curriculum objectives are not well defined. If they were, the decision would be based strictly on a set of performance and compatibility requirements and not a comparison of speeds and feeds.

When you look at these two trends under separate lights, it becomes very easy to deal with them. Not necessarily cheap or easy to manage, but easier to understand.

ONE-TO-ONE: A NEW CONCEPT FOR AN OLD BUZZWORD

We discussed this concept in our previous book, *N3xt Practices*, but it warrants some attention in the vision discussion.

One thing that's become clear is that there is no single correct model for 1:1 initiatives. And the reality is that those initiatives that fail to meet their desired outcomes probably weren't clearly defined from the start.

Unless, of course, the objective is merely to put technology in the hands of students and hope that they will figure it out from there. That is a typical case of a solution looking for a problem!

We believe in looking at 1:1 in a new way. It is not about one student, one device. It is about one teacher to one student. It's about the number of times during the day a teacher has meaningful contact with a student, whether through a text message, a comment exchange in Google Docs, or a face-to-face encounter.

Technology has provided a means for creating extra time for a teacher to collaborate in a more meaningful way with students, and that is the most powerful thing that an effective 1:1 program brings to the table.

ONE-TO-ONE COMPLEXITY

Three areas of complexity need to be considered for any 1:1 initiative: performance and reliability, administration and maintenance, and nontechnical considerations.

As you move on a continuum from nonmobile computer labs, to thin clients, to laptops, to netbooks or mini laptops, to tablets, to smart phones (BYOD), you will note the following:

- *Performance and reliability decrease.* Fat PCs with monitors will provide the highest performance and stability for each dollar. As you move toward mobile devices, such as tablets and smartphones, the amount of computing power decreases. Administering a variety of operating systems reduces overall system reliability.
- *Administration and maintenance increase.* PCs and laptops in the wired lab are easier to administer and maintain. As you move to wireless and varied operating systems, administration becomes more complex.
- *Nontechnical considerations increase.* Nontechnical considerations include decisions about whether to purchase insurance or self-insure, who will own the devices, what to do in cases of loss or theft, board policy, and acceptable use policies.

CHAPTER 6

Infrastructure

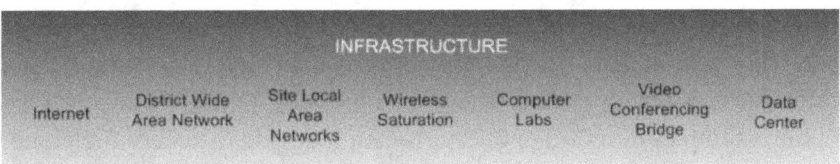

Figure 6.1

As we discuss the lower-level infrastructure, it becomes important to understand that the infrastructure systems and technologies encompassed in the vision cost significant amounts of money, and it's mostly hidden in the ground and behind the walls.

In other words, the money being spent for classroom technologies is seen and felt in the classrooms by the teachers and students. Conversely, network infrastructure for local and wireless networking is installed within the walls and buildings, completely invisible to the end user (if done correctly).

That means more than half the cost of your curricular initiative—if it requires mobility and 1:1—will likely need to be spent first and will be invisible to the teachers and students.

INTERNET

The Internet—your pathway to the outside world of *everything*—is truly that. We contend that every school district in the United States is now totally dependent on the Internet for business and curricular operations.

Payroll, e-mail, security, teacher webpages, student storage and devices, and content websites—every aspect of school operations has become at least predominantly dependent on the Internet.

It's truly the district's lifeline to the outside world. And, as your wireless device count expands and 1:1 and BYOD initiatives take hold, you can bank on an exponential expansion in bandwidth required, both at the LAN network core (10Gbps) and out to the Internet. You can also bank on your Internet filter needing to be upgraded and redundant.

Larger districts will need at least two separate connections to the Internet for load balancing and to provide primary/secondary fail-over for critical applications.

What this means to district leadership and the vision is that every component in the infrastructure platform list needs support resources and life-cycle budget—read support staff, maintenance contracts, and future dollars for replacement.

For example, if you give every student a device to access the cloud, then the cloud must be available via any wireless network they may be accessing. But if you don't build the infrastructure to deliver the cloud, then neither platform will work as intended. Think if you purchased every student a car but didn't build any roads or gas stations.

WIDE AREA NETWORK

Your district's wide area network (WAN) is the extension of each site's network to the district office and pathway to the Internet. Just as the addition of wireless access points will exponentially increase the bandwidth requirement at the LAN core to 10Gbps, the WAN connectivity bandwidth requirement to the district core and to the Internet will increase similarly.

The most important consideration is that whatever you've got now will likely not be enough in another year. And this won't peak until you're supporting multiple devices for each user.

The other strategic implication with your WAN is that it is likely a service with monthly fees. Unless your district is lucky enough to have access to free metropolitan fiber, you need a life-cycle budget for the routing and security equipment (redundant, of course) and a budget for the monthly services fees, which will easily exceed the capital outlay.

The good news is that your district has been doing this already; just get ready for the impending capital costs and service rate increases.

VIDEO CONFERENCING

We discussed earlier the concept of virtual classrooms, but we often merely consider the scenario closest to our experience and requirements. However, to build a facility that is flexible enough to support more than just a couple of models can be very expensive and difficult to define.

Remote interfaces are the various methods of communicating over distance using audio and video. It's easy to imagine looking at a live image of someone's face and being able to hear them speak. How about viewing documents and marking them up? How will meeting notes or recordings of the meeting be accessed later? The remote interface can simulate the level of interaction of the live synchronous classroom. The limitations, however, become obvious.

Let's take a look at some of the fundamental characteristics of the bricks-and-mortar classroom:

- This model requires that all students and teachers travel to the same physical location and arrive and stay for the same amount of time on a given schedule.
- There are functional limitations to the physical classroom, including sitting too far away (theater seating) and not being able to see and hear the same interaction as those students sitting closer.
- Distractions within the classroom, such as a disruptive student or a loud air conditioner, can render the bricks-and-mortar classroom ineffective for individual students.
- Additionally, if one student is not able to attend the synchronous lesson in person, the entire lesson, exercises, and classroom interaction are lost forever.
- Without asynchronous tools, the student must achieve another synchronous interaction with the teacher, another student, or a tutor in order to gain the lost lesson beyond written lesson plans and exercises.

A synchronous virtual classroom can take the following forms:

- A teacher and students in a bricks-and-mortar classroom with one remote student
- A teacher and students in a bricks-and-mortar classroom with a remote classroom with multiple students
- A teacher and students in a bricks-and-mortar classroom with multiple remote students
- A teacher and students in a bricks-and-mortar classroom with multiple remote classrooms with multiple students each, and/or a combination of remote classrooms and individual remote users
- A remote teacher and students in a bricks-and-mortar classroom
- A remote teacher and remote students in bricks-and-mortar classrooms and individual remote students/classrooms

The levels of functional complexity are numerous. Each scenario listed above may require various teaching styles as well as equipment. Each scenario will have varying classroom management challenges, as well as evaluation and assessment requirements.

In order to develop the solutions for your relevant scenario, first examine how the teaching and learning environment is affected by the new participants, and then determine what technical capabilities are required to support real-time interactivity between teachers and students.

Each of these solution scenarios will require some type of classroom video conferencing interface (VCI) in the local classroom and either another type of classroom VCI for a remote classroom or a single-user VCI (think Skype) or both. The VCI platform, therefore, becomes the enabling technology.

A robust VCI platform may support multiple inputs and outputs, providing flexibility regarding what will be displayed locally at each endpoint. Typical VCI platforms include two large-screen monitors or projector screens, allowing the local endpoint administrator to select between the most relevant views, such as the remote participants, a computer presentation, and/or streaming video.

The technical hardware and software to support each of the above scenarios can be complex and very expensive; thus, the specific model relevant to your individual requirements should be examined thoughtfully.

For example, connecting a single remote student to a bricks-and-mortar classroom may require a simple hardware/software combination like Skype; however, hosting a remote classroom of students may require large-scale video conferencing equipment.

Virtual classroom models that attempt to support more than just one or two of the above scenarios may be too complex for many teachers to manage. In such cases, it would be easier to build one type of virtual classroom to address a specific need than to build multiple virtual classroom facilities that could support multiple use models.

Let's take the models one at a time to understand what the basic interface between the entities might look like.

- A teacher and students in a bricks-and-mortar classroom with one remote student.

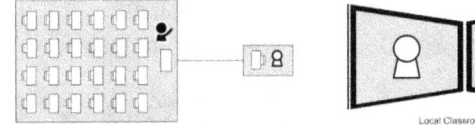

Figure 6.2

Notice that the classroom must have a VCI that will allow the remote user to see the teacher but not necessarily the other students. A second camera would be required if the remote student would also need to view of the other students.

- A teacher and students in a bricks-and-mortar classroom with a remote classroom with multiple students.

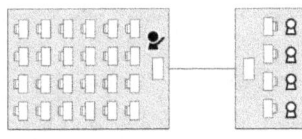

Figure 6.3

Note that the remote students will have a view of the teacher while the local students will have a view of the remote students.

A second camera would be required to allow the remote students to see the local students, although audio should be shared equally.

- A teacher and students in a bricks-and-mortar classroom with multiple remote students.

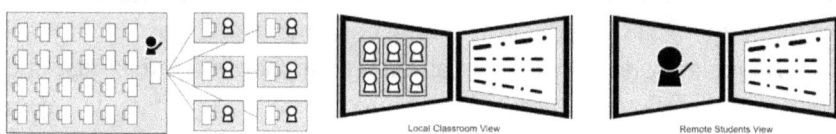

Figure 6.4

Note that once more than one remote site is considered, a new video conferencing bridge technology will become necessary. This multipoint bridge is not only costly but also requires special software for managing the VCI. This scenario may lead to considering a cloud-based VCI service.

- A teacher and students in a bricks-and-mortar classroom with multiple remote classrooms with multiple students each, and/or a combination of remote classrooms and individual remote users

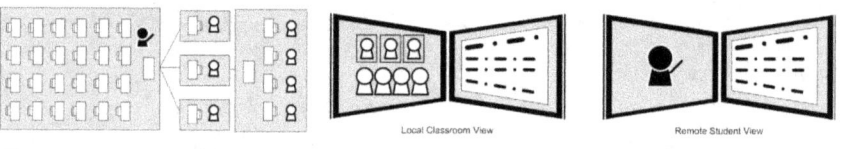

Figure 6.5

- A remote teacher and students in a bricks-and-mortar classroom

Figure 6.6

- A remote teacher and remote students in bricks-and-mortar classrooms and individual remote students and/or classrooms

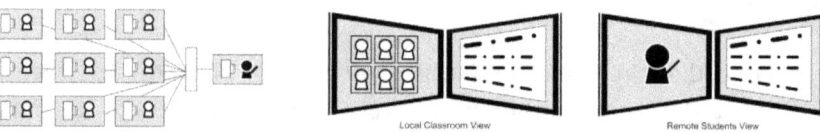

Figure 6.7

Leader Led

All traditional (bricks-and-mortar) as well as nontraditional learning models tend to be leader led. This does not change in the virtual classroom. Limitations may come into play when synchronous interaction is required.

Obviously, the leader-led model is not in effect 100 percent of the time. Interactivity and project-based curricula will undoubtedly provide opportunities for individual students, groups of students, and possibly guests to lead specific discussions and activities.

The more that is known about these other activities, the better the designer will be able to model each scenario and provide the appropriate hardware and software to support the model.

Remote Teacher

The remote teacher is easy to visualize. Instead of seeing a live teacher, the students see a view of the teacher on the big screen in the front of the class. The teacher in his or her remote studio would have the same full technology and media access as a local teacher and would be able to control what the students view.

For instance, the remote teacher would be able to use a document camera in exactly the same way it might be used in the classroom. The teacher would see a view of the students and hear them via a shared microphone.

You can see that this scenario would work best with two screens to allow students to see the teacher and the projected multimedia.

Remote Students

Remote students are not as easy to visualize. The first layer of complexity comes with a classroom with one remote student.

To provide the remote student with a full interactive scene requires a view of the teacher, a view of the classroom, and a third view of the projected media (computer or video screen).

This example still wouldn't provide the remote student a similar interaction with the other students since the remote student would see a view of the classroom as if he were the teacher, and vice versa.

The second layer of complexity involves multiple remote students and then a mixture of remote individuals and remote classrooms.

Each model requires more complex technology, and all fail to truly simulate the classroom experience.

WIRELESS SATURATION

There are two different models to consider when building a wireless infrastructure. One model is a wireless network that provides "coverage," and the other is a "saturated" wireless network.

We discussed this at length in our previous book *(N3xt Practices)*, but suffice it to say that with 1:1 and BYOD initiatives, saturation is your objective.

Imagine if you were crossing a river in a rowboat. When two or three people get in the rowboat, the chances of them successfully crossing the river is pretty high. If thirty people all jumped in the rowboat, the chances of a successful crossing are slim to none. The rowboat becomes overwhelmed and can't function effectively.

Wired networks (copper and fiber optic) have a funny way of working wonderfully for the first few users and then crashing and burning once the whole school tries to connect. The same goes for wireless.

Think of the teacher that installed his or her own wireless access point to support some classroom laptops. If every teacher now did the same thing, the whole network would grind to a halt—guaranteed. And the cost to do the implementation correctly may be two to three times the expected cost because of additional power, cabling, network equipment, and management hardware and software required for a campus-wide wireless network.

In a saturated wireless model you would survey your campus and all of the buildings taking into consideration *how many* devices can connect to the wireless network from any physical location. A saturated wireless network allows for many devices to connect to the wireless network and can support an influx of many new devices entering the same physical space.

Using today's newest optimized wireless technologies, access points in a saturated environment can detect when neighboring access points are under heavy demand; they will automatically adjust their antennas to support the additional demand and/or pass connections to a nearby access point that has spare capacity.

Building a saturated wireless environment costs more, but with testing, BYOD, and 1:1 curriculum initiatives proliferating, the bandwidth required will escalate exponentially.

Many IT practitioners now deploy one access point in every classroom to ensure a viable wireless network connection and consider putting two network cables in the ceiling for a future additional access point (or one that requires two drops).

COMPUTER LABS

The funny thing is, as maligned as the traditional computer lab has become, it still has a role within the educational environment. The relevant questions are the following:

1. Do all students still need their own computers for the entire class period, or has that been solved by our 1:1 or BYOD initiative?
2. Can we just provide one laptop to each student in the regular classroom (or do we need to have a special room called the computer lab)?
3. Is there a need for special or high-end equipment (it is common to have special equipment for photography, graphic arts, CAD, software development, and so forth)?
4. How is the computer lab staffed?

Once again, the curriculum objective provides the need. No need? No stuff.

COMPUTERS ON WHEELS (COWS)

COWs are actually the answer to question number 2 above. If access to all curriculum software can be provided by rolling in a number of laptops, then COWs may be an alternative to the traditional computer lab.

But COWs bring with them their own special set of questions and requirements, such as the following:

- Where will the COWs be stored? Is there enough power available, and is it accessible to all teachers who will use it?
- How many classrooms are sharing the COWs?

- How will the COWs be reserved for use?
- Can the COWs realistically be rolled from the storage location to the classroom?
- Who is responsible for the maintenance and charging of the laptops?
- Do we have wireless saturation in every location where the COWs may be used?
- Also, COWs probably won't eliminate the need for labs mentioned in question number 3 above.
- And so on and so forth.

Sorry. We didn't mean to bum you out with the issues with implementing COWs, or mobile labs. We just want you to be aware of the implementation issues because they will affect the overall scope and scale of your educational technology vision.

CHAPTER 7

Support and Sustainability

Sustainability is a great buzzword for *keeping things running*, but it is very relevant to technology systems in education. We see technology sustainability in the following contexts: the effective use of technology systems to support the end product (classroom curriculum enhancement), the effective support and maintenance of the technology systems, and the life cycle of use for technology replacement.

EDUCATIONAL TECHNOLOGY SERVICES

We've already discussed the role of educational technology services within the organization. In the context of sustainability, we can see once again there must be a proactive, as well as a reactive, response team.

The proactive scope is the professional development program. The educational technology professional development curriculum is based around indoctrination and guidance in all the district standard suites. Examples follow.

The reactive scope includes the help desk response categories specific to instructional suites and applications and their use.

For instance, if a teacher calls the help desk for taking attendance, or using the LMS, the call-tracking system should assign the call to the educational technology support person, not the desktop support technician.

PROFESSIONAL DEVELOPMENT

Professional development isn't just teacher training or a teacher on special assignment (TOSA). Professional development must produce and evaluate the following base-level competencies:

- Classroom technology suite
  - Computer, wireless, and Internet
  - Computer OS and productivity suite
  - LMS access and use
- Classroom administrative applications
  - Attendance
  - Gradebook
- LMS system
  - Content development

INFORMATION TECHNOLOGY SERVICES

We've already discussed these areas at length in the information technology platforms section. In the context of sustainability, it is important to consider what it will take not only to achieve each department's objectives but also to maintain and support the entire IT enterprise, including its own internal resources.

And guess what? It's another "put your money where your mouth is" scenario.

Every one of the staff members within the IT organization requires his or her own tools, certifications, training, and occupational support. Some of these are annualized budgets, training budgets, trade shows, manuals, and certification testing.

These are your frontline technology advocates. They need tools and organizational support just like the rest of your organization. Don't forget them.

TECHNOLOGY REFRESH

This may be the most unaddressed area in educational technology—even more so than BC/DR (business continuity and disaster recovery). Technology refresh is the process, planning, and *funding* to maximize the useful life of technology equipment and devices and to mitigate large-scale obsolescence and critical replacement.

The concept is very straightforward: following any large-scale technology deployment, plan for the obsolescence and refresh of 25 percent to 35 percent of the installed base of computing (and network) equipment.

A process also known as "technology life cycle" insures that old technology is taken out of service within its functional life cycle. For most equipment this is from three to five years. However, with lower-cost and more quickly changing technology, it is two to four years.

Many equity and access issues will arise as you attempt to forestall current investments in technology in order to budget for future years.

Technology life cycle also warrants a discussion of technology funding and whether to lease or buy. We've included this discussion from *N3xt Practices* to highlight the salient points.

Remember the lease-versus-buy analysis you learned in Finance 101? The one thing you learned for sure was that, in real dollars, you pay a premium for financing. It isn't until you make the Net Present Value (NPV) calculation that the analysis comes to equilibrium.

But the reality is that there is always a hybrid solution presenting itself as another cost alternative. And soft-dollar costs become difficult to quantify unless you can account for dedicated staffing and resources.

OPEX VERSUS CAPEX

The reality is that if you were to examine costs over the life of the technology, the annualized operating expense (OpEx) is at a slight premium to the capital expense (CapEx) if you purchased the equipment all at one time, supported it with your own people, and depreciated it over three to five years.

Technology refresh can be your saving grace, but it may also be the sword you fall on. Not investing enough in the near term can cause a lack of acceptance and an overall unsuccessful deployment of a new technology.

Can you defend the decision to exclude a certain school or grade level from an initiative in order to refresh technology in successive years?

Do the same teachers get the refreshed technology?

Have fun developing your watertight justifications.

CONCLUSION

Vision
Final Thoughts

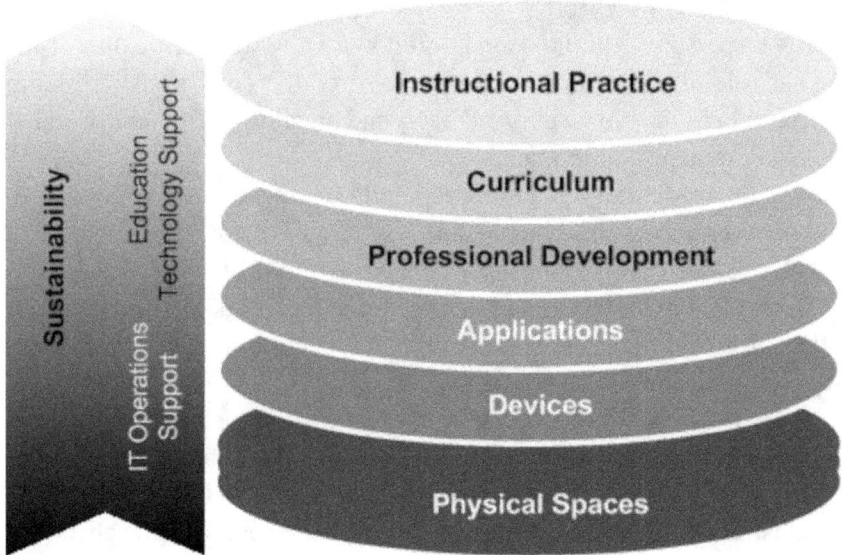

Figure D01.1

Here we are at the end of the discussion about developing a vision for educational technology. We asked earlier why educational technology needs a vision? I don't *need* a vision for plumbing. But you do *have* a vision for plumbing—plumbing should enable us to wash and use the facilities and access clean hot and cold water whenever necessary.

If you don't get it, think about the last time you went camping, visited a third-world country, or visited a very old building (built before the 1900s). You could certainly see that the builders had a much different vision for plumbing than we do today.

But it is not enough just to have a vision. The second-most-important part is *communication*—how is the vision communicated throughout the organization *and* how often?

As an example, consider the fire drill. In a school, the principal, staff, and teachers are all trained about the fire drill—exit routes, emergency communications, gathering spots, and so on.

Now consider the fire drill in a navy submarine, where seconds can mean the demise of the whole boat and all aboard.

Every single person aboard the navy submarine knows exactly what to do and his or her responsibilities in the case of fire. Each also knows and can do any other job.

Every person from the captain on down knows the criticality of his or her role. The fire drill is the exercise of the crew's vision of fire safety aboard the navy sub. And everyone practices it frequently and at the most unexpected moments.

Once your district has developed and documented the vision, communication and reinforcement must be from the top down and on a regular basis—just like the navy submarine fire drill.

It should be the basis of day-to-day decision making and guide all efforts for each individual's operational objective. Leadership *will* set the example.

I was lucky enough to speak at a recent district technology fair with a teacher from a district that I had helped develop a technology vision (the process we used is memorialized in this book). He is currently the site instructional technology liaison (ITL); he supports site teachers and acts as the site liaison to district technology meetings.

I had not met this teacher before, but he had the vision document that I had worked on with the district leadership months earlier.

I was intrigued to hear him describe the district's ed tech vision (I hadn't told him about my involvement in the model's development) and relate it to his daily teaching and liaison functions. I later asked him several questions via e-mail: What is your role (as site technology guru) in communicating the vision to others? Is this responsibility in line with your day-to-day activities? How do you see it affecting (or not affecting) your day-to-day interactions with the teachers you support? This was his response:

> Yes, this responsibility is in line with my day-to-day activities and serves to anchor the daily implementation of education technology within my classroom. I see the vision statement as a helpful reference guide in leading my colleagues toward a clearer understanding as to how technology integration in the classroom is now a vital part of equipping students for success in an increasingly technology-driven postsecondary environment.
>
> Ben Wallace, fourth grade, Avaxat Elementary

Having both a clear, articulated vision about how technology supports your instructional practice and a coherent communication plan will give you the platform from which to successfully create an environment that supports twenty-first-century learning. The fundamentals of students—communicating, collaborating, critical thinking, and creativity—are anchored in your district's educational technology vision.

About the Authors

Darryl Vidal has been consulting for schools implementing technology for over twenty years and has a bachelor's degree in information management. He started his technical career installing ethernet networks at Hughes Aircraft and other aerospace firms in the early 1980s. After working at Apple Computer with education accounts in the late 1980s, he began technical consulting for school districts. His projects have included district-wide implementations of VoIP, wireless, desktop and data center virtualization, and video security. His primary instructional focus for over fifteen years has been the ever-evolving technology classroom. Mr. Vidal has developed the formal strategic planning and project management methodology known as MAPit. He is currently vice president and principal education technology consultant for Southern California–based consultancy Network Solutions.

Michael Casey has over thirty years of experience in education as a classroom teacher, educational technology resource teacher, program manager for educational technology, and executive director for information technology at San Diego Unified School District. Mr. Casey has taught chemistry, physics, mathematics, and computer science at the secondary levels. He also taught at the university level at San Diego State University and the University of California, San Diego Extension College. His accomplishments include enterprise implementations of enterprise resource planning (ERP) solutions in human resources; finance; supply chains; student information systems; data warehousing; Microsoft Collaboration Tools; video conferencing; and enterprise wireless and special-education solutions. He is nationally recognized for successful ERP implementations and has reviewed numerous implementations for the Council of the Great City Schools. He is currently the director of technology for Del Mar Union Schools and the president and CEO of Eire Group, a technology-consulting solutions group.

www.ingramcontent.com/pod-product-compliance
Lightning Source LLC
Chambersburg PA
CBHW051815230426
43672CB00012B/2750